QUIET ACHIEVER

.

QUIET ACHIEVER

The Life and Times of Tan Sri Dr Tan Chin Tuan

Mike Macbeth

TIMES EDITIONS

© Mike Macbeth 2003
Published by Times Editions
An imprint of Times Media Pte Ltd
A member of the Times International Publishing Group
1 New Industrial Road
Singapore 536196
Tel: (65) 6213 9288 Fax: (65) 6285 4871
E-mail: te@tpl.com.sg
Online bookstore: http://www.timesone.com.sg/te

Times Subang
Lot 46, Subang Hi-Tech Industrial Park
Batu Tiga, 40000 Shah Alam
Selangor Darul Ehsan, Malaysia
Tel & Fax: (603) 5636 3517
E-mail: cchong@tpg.com.my

National Library Board (Singapore) Cataloguing in Publication Data
Macbeth, Mike.
    Quiet Achiever: The Life and Times of Tan Sri Dr Tan Chin Tuan / Mike Macbeth.
— Singapore : Times Editions, 2002.
    p. cm.
    ISBN : 981-232-198-5
1. Tan, Chin Tuan, Tan Sri, 1908-
2. Bankers —Singapore —Biography.
I. Title.
HG1552   332.1092 — dc21   SLS2002015777

Printed by Utopia Press Pte Ltd

Contents

Acknowledgements

No meaningful biography is possible without the co-operation of its subject. First and foremost, I am indebted to Tan Sri Dr Tan Chin Tuan, who generously spent many hours with the writer. With a razor sharp and focused mind, his effortless ability to recall names, dates and minute details, vitalised his story. TCT also made available historical documents, business data and other research materials, invaluable to the compilation of the book.

I also appreciate the generosity of his family for their continued guidance and support, particularly TCT's daughter, Mrs Choo Campbell, and granddaughter, Chew Gek Khim. Thank you also to TCT's nephew Dr Tony Tan Keng Yam, who granted an interview during his tenure with the OCBC.

The book would have been impossible to write without the co-operation of Tan Sri's able staff, particularly Cecilia Chua and Chu Tee Chui, who miraculously and effortlessly knew where to instantly find materials that spanned more than 50 years. I am indebted to Dr Kevin Tan (former associate professor, Faculty of Law, National University of Singapore) for his wisdom and guidance, particularly in the final stages of the writing. I am also grateful to historian Lee Su Yin, for confirming endless historical facts and offering excellent suggestions.

Finally, special appreciation to John Burke for his encouragement and assistance in helping me comprehend the details of the myriad corporate and business undertakings, and to my editors at Times Media Pte Ltd, Richard Jeremy Davies and Melvin Neo, for their patience, judgement and sagacity.

Any inspiration generated by the example of this extraordinary life is appropriately credited to the great banker and philanthropist himself, Tan Sri Dr Tan Chin Tuan. Any errors or omissions are entirely the fault of the writer.

Author's Foreword

From time to time, as senior writer of *Canadian Business Magazine*, I heard stories of a famous banker in Singapore with a contradictory reputation. Revered by some, criticised by others, his admirers and detractors only agreed (albeit sometimes grudgingly) on one abiding response to this man's character — universal respect.

Those who had business dealings with him over the years had described him paradoxically as brilliant, powerful, obstinate, fair, shrewd, perceptive, tough, kind, inflexible, generous, stubborn and astute. How could one man evoke such a range of opinions and impressions?

Eventually, I was invited to meet this enigma. Waiting in the ante-room of his executive offices on the 49th floor of the impressive OCBC Centre in Singapore's business district, I was both intrigued and apprehensive, expecting a man of such wealth and influence to be imperious and difficult.

A hush came over the room as he entered, a strange phenomenon usually associated with royalty. And, with the accomplished ease of the nobility, my host was disarming and gracious. A compelling storyteller of considerable charm and wit, he described, over tea served on delicate china, and later at a sumptuous ten-course luncheon, some of the events of his dramatic life. Captivated, his potential biographer welcomed the opportunity to tell his story.

The task is impossible. He is not one book — his life speaks volumes. Others will detail his leadership roles in banking, industry and transitional politics. The following is simply an overview of a life well lived — an appetiser for the main course of work that someday will do historical justice to his multi-faceted contributions to commerce, politics and society.

In many ways, the life of Tan Sri Dr Tan Chin Tuan mirrors the young nation he helped build. Singapore's metamorphosis from a post-war colonial outpost to an economic powerhouse took only four (albeit turbulent) decades. Her subservience through British colonialism and Japanese occupation has ended. Today she serves no masters.

Prior to World War II, Tan Chin Tuan, like all Chinese in Singapore, was virtually a second-class citizen in his own country. However, he displayed a unique ability to gracefully cross all cultural barriers. Despite colonial prejudice, the British admired and trusted him. Through his actions, words and deeds, TCT (the informal sobriquet by which he is universally known) gained the confidence of the colonial government before and during the Second World War. After the war, he rose to the highest public office that could be held by an Asian at the time, that of Deputy President of the Legislative Council. His ability to forge positive relationships with both the British and Chinese community helped smooth the early years of Singapore's transition from a colony to independent nationhood.

Although TCT's contributions to public life ended in 1955, his banking and business influence continued to accelerate. His familiarity with Western business practices and concepts, such as public companies, and his warm relationship with the British, presented him with the opportunity to invest in almost every sector of the economy as the British withdrew. The corporations he guided included The Straits Trading Company Ltd, The Great Eastern Life Assurance Co Ltd, Malayan Breweries Ltd, Fraser & Neave Ltd, Robinson & Co Ltd, Raffles Hotel, and The Overseas Assurance Corporation Ltd.

Under his stewardship, the Oversea-Chinese Banking Corporation became one of the world's most illustrious and wealthy banks. On the day of his retirement in 1983, OCBC's market capitalisation exceeded

$5.3 billion, more than the Midland and Westpac banks combined. This figure represented five times shareholders' funds, underlining the value of its shares and demonstrating the esteem and confidence the investing public had in OCBC.

Tan Chin Tuan has been described as the embodiment of the Oversea-Chinese Banking Corporation. Even if today the OCBC is no longer Singapore's largest bank, the story of Tan Chin Tuan's stewardship is significant. However, the list of his achievements obscures the obstacles and very real dangers he endured. His life has not been easy but he never shirked the challenges confronting him. Throughout his career, Tan Chin Tuan courageously accepted what he considered necessary risks. Sometimes he also stubbornly incurred unnecessary risks, often jeopardising his own safety.

TCT's sense of justice often made things difficult for him. He would speak out when lesser men remained silent. Over his lifetime, he would try the patience of the authorities, because he refused to compromise on issues of principle. His wisdom and perceptive understanding of human nature often resulted in changes made gracefully and courteously, through diplomacy, not violence. Yet his resolve and spirit, though fierce, was tempered with gentility.

An admirer once noted that he had all the attributes of a fighting cock — determination, fearlessness and tenacity. He replied, "I would rather be a cock that fights than a cock that crows."

Tan Sri Dr Tan Chin Tuan PSM CBE JP Hon LLD Hon D Litt is not a man to crow. Despite the honours and decorations that have been bestowed upon him, he remains modest. An intensely private man, he seeks no public recognition for his achievements and contributions. A compassionate benefactor, he quietly funds several major foundations dedicated to helping those in need. Even at the age of 94, still sharp and vital, he takes an active interest in his charities, in the world of business and finance and in the affairs of state.

Tan Chin Tuan's life story forms a bridge between colonial Singapore and today's modern city-state. Born into a time of inequality, he and those of his generation helped guide the changes that transformed his nation's commerce, politics and society. Singapore's history would be incomplete without the stories of men of integrity like Tan Chin Tuan, who had the will to seek their own destiny and the courage to fight for what is right.

Mike Macbeth
December, 2002

The Early Years

The morning began as predictably as all Singapore mornings. A cacophony of sounds intertwined as the city awoke. The soft air vibrated with the rumble of carriages, squeaking wagons, clattering carts, clopping hooves and growling automobiles. Rival roosters crowed incessantly in futile competition, oblivious to the symphony of commerce.

On this bustling Saturday in the sixth month of 1922, the staff of the bank on Chulia Street began their working day. The massive front door was thrown open by the night watchman. The staff quietly filed in and took their places. Engrossed in their preparations, they hardly noticed a thirteen-year-old boy who suddenly entered the bank. Familiar with the routine, the youth proceeded directly to the vault in the basement.

In the vault, the boy withdrew a key from his pocket. Three keys were required to open the bank's strong room. The bank's general manager had been unavoidably delayed, so he entrusted his key to his son. Deputising for his father, the youth and two other bank officers, each with complementary keys, unlocked the strong room door. They entered the strong room, where the chief cashier withdrew the estimated cash needed for the day. After noting the amount withdrawn in a book, they returned to the ground floor where the bank tellers were waiting. The Oversea-Chinese Bank was open for business.

That incident was symbolic of things to come. The youth with the key would one day enjoy an illustrious banking career of his own. He would guide his bank through war, national reconstruction, colonial withdrawal, unprecedented economic growth, technological revolution and globalisation. As chairman, he would become the key to the success of the Oversea-Chinese Banking Corporation. By the time of his retirement in 1983, OCBC would become the largest bank in Singapore. His fifty-eight-year career with the bank, plus his stewardship of many of Singapore's most prominent corporations, would be unprecedented.

Of equal importance would be his unheralded contributions to the establishment of modern-day Singapore and to the Chinese community. Achieved quietly and unobtrusively, these would become his enduring gifts to the history of his country.

A natural leader, both the bank and his nation would turn to him in their time of need. But on this June morning of 1922, the future Tan Sri Dr Tan Chin Tuan PSM CBE JP Hon LLD Hon D Litt was known to the bank employees simply as Chin Tuan, son of Tan Cheng Siong.

The Singapore of the post-Victorian era that Tan Chin Tuan was born into was a starched colony, where the Chinese majority and the ruling British minority lived in isolation, side by side, rarely interacting.

The romantic writings of Kipling, Conrad and Maugham depicted to the outside world an exotic British enclave, evoking images of ancient spice routes, soft ocean breezes, waving palms, white parasols and silk cravats. Asians were seldom acknowledged by this colonial society. But during Tan Chin Tuan's adult life, the British hold on the steamy city-state would evaporate into history and memories.

This 650-sq.-km. island south of the Malay Peninsula would evolve into a thriving, dynamic city. Comfortably merging the ancient cultures of China, India and the Malay Archipelago with the advanced technologies of the West, modern Singapore would become not just an intermediary between East and West, but also the prosperous beneficiary of the best of both worlds.

Although lacking in natural resources, Singapore's key geographic location and industrious labour force combined to establish a robust trading, financial and redistribution centre for Southeast Asia. United in purpose, its people of different races and origins forged a vigorous, harmonious union. Economically and politically, the city-state gradually assumed an international importance belying its size.

Singapore's ultimate success stemmed from its geographical and commercial importance. Heavy colonisation by the British, French, Dutch and Spanish in Southeast Asia increased trade in the region. The opening of the Suez Canal in 1869 established the Straits of Malacca as the major waterway between Europe and the East.

As steam ships replaced tall sailing ships, and world demand for rubber, tin and other commodities spiralled, Singapore's deep natural harbour became crucial to the region's economy. By the turn of the century, Singapore was Asia's most cosmopolitan city with more than 200,000 inhabitants of Chinese, Malay, Sumatran, Javanese, Indian, Arabic, Jewish, Eurasian and European descent.

Although the rubber boom had begun in the later years of the nineteenth century, the discovery of vulcanisation — by adding sulphur to the rubber — led to unlimited commercial applications. Footwear, clothing and bumpers for railway cars required vast quantities of rubber. Following the development of the internal combustion engine, the rapid growth of the automobile industry at the beginning of the new century hungrily consumed the world's sources of rubber.

As rubber prices soared, entrepreneurs quickly secured acres of arable land and cleared the Malayan jungle to satisfy the seemingly insatiable demand for the sticky latex. In 1910, world consumption of crude rubber was 100,000 tons. By 1920, it had tripled, and Malaya led the world in rubber production.

British banks served European customers and commerce. Locally, three banks were established during this decade to take advantage of the booming world market for rubber and tin, and to serve the Hokkien community, which commercially and numerically dominated the Chinese population of Singapore. The Chinese Commercial Bank Ltd was founded first in 1912, followed by the Ho Hong Bank Ltd in 1917 and the Oversea-Chinese Bank Ltd in 1919.

Economic and political power, however, was held firmly by the British. As Singapore's strategic and commercial importance grew, the British grip on the island tightened.

This was the Singapore Tan Chin Tuan was born into on November 21, 1908. His mother, Lee Guay Eng, was locally born. His father, Tan Cheng Siong, had emigrated from China and was a naturalised British subject.

Tan Cheng Siong was a prominent Hokkien businessman, who owned several sawmills and a rubber estate on the east coast of Johore. An inspiring role model, he served as Justice of the Peace, a member of both the Chinese Chamber of Commerce and the Chinese Advisory Board, and as honorary president of the Tan Clan — community positions which eventually his son would also hold.

Tan Cheng Siong was also the consummate banker, universally respected and admired. Until 1921, he had been a member of the board of directors of the Oversea-Chinese Bank. However, when the bank's general manager suddenly died, Cheng Siong resigned from the board and took on this post as he was the late general manager's guarantor. In doing so, he set a precedent by being the bank's first non-English educated general manager.

Tan Chin Tuan's childhood was idyllic. He would often accompany his father to the rubber plantation. They would travel north by car from Singapore to the Woodlands jetty. On the Johore Bahru side, they would continue northward through Kota Tinggi to a village called Mawai on the Sedili River. While waiting for the tide to rise, they would cook a meal, chatting quietly and forming the unspoken bond only a father and son can know. Once the tide swept in, their journey resumed in a small boat with an outboard motor. It would take two hours of travelling, along the Sedili River, then up the Kambau, a small tributary, to reach the estate. Upon arrival, the plantation was full of exciting possibilities for adventure, exploration and nature study, in jungle trails or on the river. It had been a gambier and pepper growing settlement in the nineteenth century and, far more exotically for a little boy, a pirate's lair.

The family enjoyed all the conveniences of the early twentieth century. Tan Chin Tuan's father was one of the first to obtain a telephone. To place a call, the handle on the side was cranked once. The phone didn't always work and after several attempts at turning the handle, a frustrated Cheng Siong would ask his son to run to the home of the person he was calling and request that they pick up the phone.

Tan Cheng Siong was also often frustrated by another handle — that of the car he had purchased. He hired an immense Bengali chauffeur with the requisite strength to crank the car to start it. If the car backfired, the crankshaft could kick back and break a man's arm. The Indian would start the car and then hold it as the chugging vehicle attempted to move. Then he would quickly jump behind the steering wheel, before, inevitably, the car stalled. Later the family upgraded to a more reliable Page. The only lighting available for the automobiles of the day was carbide lamps, which would be snuffed out by each gust of wind. TCT (his initials would become as identifiable as his name) impressed his father when he resourcefully combined a wet battery with some wires and a bulb, and fashioned a headlight for the car.

Mature beyond his years and given the responsibility of an adult, TCT participated in many aspects of Cheng Siong's business life, from the rubber plantation to the bank. Tan Chin Tuan's famed entrepreneurial spirit might have been sparked by another of Cheng Siong's business ventures.

Tan Cheng Siong was one of the businessmen appointed by the government to handle the distribution of rice during the period of shortages after World War I. The precious rice was obtained from the official stores and then sold in shops on a rationed basis. Each person was entitled to one bag of rice. As the rice was repacked into smaller bags, some grains quite naturally spilled to the ground. Young Chin Tuan disliked seeing waste and looked for a creative way to exploit it. He purchased some chickens to eat this rice. Unfortunately, he grew rather attached to his brood and, as they grew in size and number, refused to allow his family to slaughter the birds for food. But fate soon intervened with a resolution to the household impasse — the chickens developed a fatal disease and the entire flock succumbed.

Demonstrating paternal affection and pride, Tan Cheng Siong took Chin Tuan with him when he went to his clubs. Singapore had three main clubs for the wealthy of the Chinese community, the premier being the Ee Hoe Hean. The Straits-born usually joined the Weekly Entertainment Club and the China-born, mostly merchants, frequented the Goh Loo Club. The Goh Loo Club and the Ee Hoe Hean Club, both located in the aptly named Club Street, served as fashionable gathering places where Hokkien businessmen met to exchange stories, obtain news of China and talk business. Although there were few pleasures here for a child (except the delicious foods) and little opportunities for play, Chin Tuan was quiet and well-behaved.

It was sometimes difficult for a little boy, only nine or ten years old, to sit patiently while his father engaged in conversation. But the lessons learned and the contacts made in these exclusive clubs were invaluable.

Tan Chin Tuan quickly learned the manners, customs and traditions of the adult Chinese business world. More importantly, he met and got to know his father's friends — the elite of this society. The most prominent of these, the renowned business leader and philanthropist Tan Kah Kee, would play a pivotal role in TCT's early banking career and in his political life.

TCT's parents were born into a time when most Chinese living in Singapore, if educated at all, would be taught in the Chinese language. Only a small minority of the Chinese population had a formal education or learned to speak or write English. Cheng Siong supported all forms of education, recognising that a knowledge of English could allow businessmen to cross the cultural barrier and work with the British. Yet, like his friend Tan Kah Kee, Tan Cheng Siong also encouraged and supported the Chinese schools by financing them and sitting on their management committees. Although it was assumed he would send his son to a Chinese school, he did not.

Tan Cheng Siong was unusual for a man of his time. He was remarkably open to Western ideas. Although he ran his household as conservatively and authoritatively as most Chinese businessmen, he accepted certain Western medical practices, for example, allowing a female dentist to treat his wife.

During the course of several house calls to their long and narrow shophouse in Japan Street (later renamed Boon Tat Street), the dentist took a particular interest in Chin Tuan. She suggested to his mother that he should attend her own alma mater, the Methodist Girls' School. These recommendations were reinforced by the suggestions of the prominent Methodist missionary, Miss Sophia Blackmore, who founded the Methodist Girls' School. Tan Cheng Siong met and came to respect Miss Blackmore. He thus opened his door and his mind to the Methodist missionaries and educationists, who were setting their sights on the Chinese community.

Sophia Blackmore was a rare and rather dramatic sight. She had been making home visits in the Telok Ayer area long before Chin Tuan was born. Arriving in a pony-drawn carriage, this young white woman routinely inspired curiosity and ritualistic larceny. While she was inside the shophouses, sharing the word of the gospel, mischievous locals stealthily shared her possessions. A particular favourite was her lace parasols.

Miss Blackmore had also started a home for orphans, which supplemented its income by accepting paid boarders. Like many of its counterparts in Britain, the Nind Home School permitted young male students in the junior classrooms. She persuaded Tan Cheng Siong to allow the seven-year-old Chin Tuan to take lessons in English there as a day student.

Nind Home School became a daily destination for both Chin Tuan and his mother, who also attended Miss Blackmore's classes. After a few months, Chin Tuan was transferred to the Methodist Girls' School, where he met and befriended another boy, the future doctor, surgeon and President of the Republic of Singapore, Benjamin Sheares. The new school also provided an introduction to a pretty schoolgirl whom TCT often teased. Her name was Helene Wee — his future bride.

Four years later, Chin Tuan was transferred from the primary school to a private boys school, the Anglo-Chinese School. He intended to complete his secondary schooling in Singapore before attending law school in Britain. It was common in the early decades of the twentieth century, for the sons of wealthy residents of Singapore to be sent to England to further their education. It was also common for these young men, away from their families' watchful eye, to succumb to the temptations of pleasure. Often, they would return home shamefaced, without a degree or diploma. TCT used to joke that the only thing these decadent youths had passed was the Suez Canal.

However, he too was slated to further his studies overseas. But fate would not grant him this opportunity. In October 1922, while still in the

Junior Cambridge class, his secure and happy childhood abruptly ended. His beloved father, Tan Cheng Siong, suffered a massive, fatal heart attack.

The sudden death of his father would ultimately affect TCT's career choice and his destiny. The immediate impact, however, was on his schooling. The prolonged funeral arrangements and ceremonies for Tan Cheng Siong affected Chin Tuan's studies. He barely passed the Junior Cambridge qualifying examinations. Two of his four teachers, Mr H.M. Hoisington and Rev Charles Blackshear Paul, believed circumstances dictated that he should be permitted to take a supplementary exam. The other two, Mr T.G. Thomas and Rev S.M. Thevathesan, preferred to adhere to the school regulations preventing a second opportunity.

Initially, the school's principal, Rev P.L. Peach, attempted to break the deadlock by deciding that TCT should repeat his year. But Chin Tuan was adamant that he wished to sit for the exam again and declared that if this was denied him, he would leave the school. "Do you think you can pass the exam then?" Peach inquired. "I believe so," TCT assured him. Acknowledging his pupil's determination, the principal relented. "You may take the examination," he promised, "and I will help you."

The principal arranged for his supportive teacher, Rev C.B. Paul, to tutor Chin Tuan privately. However, Rev Paul's lasting contribution was not so much his coaching as the encouragement he gave. Years later, when his student became an influential businessman, Singapore would benefit from his sincere appreciation of education. One of his nation's most generous philanthropists, TCT would fund the building of schools and related educational facilities. He would also honour the memories of Rev Paul, Rev Peach and his mathematics teacher, Mr Hoisington (along with Bishop W.F. Oldham, Rev J.S. Nagle, Dr Thio Chan Bee, Rev Goh Hood Keng and Lee Hah Ing), through scholarships bequeathed in their names.

TCT passed the Junior Cambridge examination easily. After successfully completing the Senior Cambridge curriculum, Chin Tuan enrolled in the Senior Commercial class, taking advantage of his aptitude for mathematics to master bookkeeping and related subjects. His career plans were still uncertain until a chance encounter with one of his father's close and trusted friends would determine his future. See Boo Ih, the managing director of the Chinese Commercial Bank, happened to be home the day Chin Tuan and his mother paid a visit to See's wife.

See knew Tan Chin Tuan from the early days when the boy had accompanied his father everywhere and knew that he was privy to many aspects of Cheng Siong's business life. This privileged access gave TCT a solid knowledge of banking services and staff responsibilities.

Upon learning from Chin Tuan's mother that her son was graduating the following February, See Boo Ih turned to Lee Guay Eng and spoke the fateful words that would begin a remarkable career, "When your son finishes his studies, ask him to come and join us at the bank."

On March 1, 1925, a young man, a little apprehensive, stood before the Chinese Commercial Bank, reporting for work. But this was no ordinary employee. On this day, as he entered the building, Tan Chin Tuan opened the door on a career that would continue for almost six decades.

His new colleagues could be forgiven if they did not immediately perceive the potential within. The almost seventeen-year-old was quiet and somewhat shy. He was impatient to learn and had a thirst for knowledge bordering on the insatiable. He demonstrated a remarkable ability with money, with a creative entrepreneurial talent that belied his years. Disciplined in manner and mind, he devoted his leisure hours to self-education and study. His senior colleagues at the bank rewarded his efforts by presenting him with a large 1927 edition of *Webster's Dictionary*.

Although he had started as a clerk, his potential was soon recognised, and the position of assistant secretary was quickly reserved for him until he reached twenty-one, the required age of majority. A year later, he was promoted to secretary and in 1932, assistant manager.

His life was fulfilled with his marriage to Helene Wee. But this tranquillity would be short-lived. Events, unfolding internationally, would bring chaos and crisis.

Half a world away, in New York City, greed fuelled a dangerous artificial economy. A speculative feeding frenzy on Wall Street, nourished by easy credit and lust for instant riches, created paper millionaires overnight. Spiralling debts and ignorance of their consequences led to a total collapse of the stock market. The day forever known as Black Tuesday, on October 29, 1929, set off an economic crisis that reverberated around the world and ushered in a decade of uncertainty.

During the 1930s, more than half the foreign bonds traded in New York and London defaulted, as commodity prices fell. The Great Depression ravaged the car market, particularly in the United States, and the demand for Malayan tin and rubber tumbled accordingly. Foreign trade decreased from $2.3 billion in 1929 to $745 million in 1932. The currency in circulation more than halved.

In Singapore, the commodities market was decimated. Bankruptcies were endemic, and assets such as rubber estates, tin mines and residential properties plunged in value. Some of the richest men tried to average their positions using leverage. They bought and sold rubber futures as the price plummeted, frantically trying to stabilise the market. Instead, most of the millionaire rubber kings were wiped out.

As the depression continued to strangle the world economy, the Chinese community, the backbone of the economies of Singapore and Malaya, was particularly hard hit. From top to bottom, everyone was suffering.

Another crisis, closer to home and hearts, compounded the disruption caused by the Great Depression. On September 18, 1931, Japan invaded Manchuria, shattering business confidence in the Far East. Three days later, Britain acted to protect her gold reserves by abandoning the gold standard. The British government justified its action by claiming that excessive withdrawals of funds (backed by gold) from London forced its hand. The move sent shock waves throughout the financial markets. Immediately, the British pound sterling was devalued.

The news devastated the local banks in Singapore. The Ho Hong Bank, which had a large foreign exchange operation and a high pound sterling position, was hardest hit by the manoeuvre. The Oversea-Chinese Bank was also affected comparatively more than the Chinese Commercial Bank, which suffered least.

The problem was intensified as all three banks had commitments in Hong Kong and China. Here, the currency was on the silver standard, which, although stronger than the Straits currency, had echoed the pound sterling's fall. The foreign exchange catastrophe, exacerbated by the increasing number of defaulting loans by their Chinese customers, created a desperate situation for all three Hokkien banks. Something had to be done.

One man prepared to intervene and rescue the Chinese Commercial Bank in its darkest hour was Chang Kia Ngau, the general manager of the Bank of China. He visited Singapore during this crisis and met with CCB's directors. The two banks already had an existing relationship, as the Bank of China represented the Chinese Commercial Bank in foreign exchange dealings in Shanghai and Hong Kong.

Chang proved his faith by purchasing 30 per cent of the Singapore bank's shares. He was also preparing to recommend that his bank's board contribute $1 million to increase its paid-up capital, contingent on the CCB directors infusing an equivalent sum. However, the Bank of China's lifeline to the CCB became unnecessary due to another development that would not only salvage the bank's standing, but also position it, ultimately, for international prominence.

The solution was to be found not just within the boundaries of Singapore, but within the very walls of the three Hokkien banks. The directors of the Ho Hong, Oversea-Chinese and Chinese Commercial banks unanimously agreed to merge. By pooling their resources, they would bolster their strengths in order to shoulder their liabilities.

A formula to evaluate the comparative worth of the shares of each bank was agreed upon and a new name was established. On October 31, 1932, the Oversea-Chinese Banking Corporation was registered, with a paid-up capital of $10 million and a nominal capital of $40 million, the largest flotation in the history of the colony.

The elegant, white China Building, designed in the style of a Peking temple, had been completed that year to provide new but separate premises for both the CCB and the OCB. After the merger, the walls dividing the two banks were torn down to create a large banking hall. Operations were merged and modernised. Although records were kept in English, cheques were honoured in both English and Chinese and most of the staff was bilingual. The prescient benefits of combining both cultures and languages would later be instituted by all of Singapore. On January 2, 1933, the merger was complete and the Oversea-Chinese Banking Corporation opened its doors for business.

The new bank required new executive officers and a new board of directors. Lee Kong Chian, the vice-chairman of the CCB, initially proposed the amalgamation. The eighteen new directors (six from each predecessor bank) rewarded his initiative by appointing him vice-chairman of OCBC. Chee Swee Cheng of the HHB became OCBC's first chairman. The merger was a triumph for the Hokkien bankers, who demonstrated a spirit of co-operation during troubled times.

One of the first to congratulate OCBC was the general manager of the Bank of China. Chang Kia Ngau graciously relinquished his holdings in the CCB to facilitate the merger, saying: "We must consider the welfare of the overseas Chinese. We must not stand in their way."

His words impressed Tan Chin Tuan. As TCT's career accelerated, so did Chang's. He later became China's Minister of Railroads and Communications as well as governor of the Central Bank of China. Many years later, the two great bankers would become staunch friends.

Countdown to Conflict

Dramatic events in solemn boardrooms had little effect on the day to day life of OCBC's future chairman Tan Chin Tuan. Although the merger resulted in casualties among the employees of the three banks, TCT's position with the bank actually improved. Young, bright and diligent, he already knew most of the important members of the Straits-born community from the Chinese Commercial Bank. Many of the Oversea-Chinese Banking Corporation's directors were China-born and he would come to know the members of that society.

In 1933, TCT was chosen to be the manager of OCBC (Properties) and concurrently manager of a newly incorporated Oversea-Chinese Banking Corporation subsidiary, Eastern Realty Company Limited.

Eastern Realty was created to reclaim rubber estates and properties mortgaged to the bank, when the owners defaulted. Most of the holdings were in neglect and required improvements, after which they were maintained until sold. TCT was chosen by the directors to oversee this subsidiary.

After his father's death, Tan Chin Tuan profitably managed the family estate of rubber plantations and a sawmill. Although still a teenager, he quickly learned that to administer a property via long distance required trusted employees and the delegation of authority. He found an excellent European manager, Laurence Henderson, to supervise the Kambau estate.

Crime was prevalent in remote areas and it was foolhardy to pay the employees in cash. Consequently, TCT continued with a practice initiated by the previous owners of the estate — the issuing of pay dockets, which were exchangeable for the official Straits Settlement bank notes. Eventually printed on quality paper by Waterlow and Sons Ltd of England, the notes bore the picture of a man tapping rubber and were made official by an engraving of TCT's signature. Few young men could boast that their name appeared on "currency".

Henderson encountered difficulty in maintaining order on the estate. When Tan Chin Tuan's father purchased it, he hired Hokkien workers to plant the rubber trees. The Teochews, whose roots on the gambier and pepper plantation went back to the nineteenth century, resented these "newcomers". The two factions often clashed, and resentments ran high.

Being the owner, TCT was exposed to this animosity and his own life was often in danger when he visited the estate. He always carried a revolver and tried to keep awake through the night by drinking tea. Once, in the silence of the night, he heard quiet footsteps creeping outside his sleeping cubicle. His heart skipped a beat. Reaching for his gun, he jumped up to confront a man brandishing a large sword. In a split second, relief replaced fear. It was his devoted Malay chauffeur, Ali, quietly patrolling the area to protect him. "I can't sleep if you are asleep," confessed his dedicated driver. "Sleep soundly and don't worry; they won't get you. They'll have to kill me first." Having first worked for TCT's father, Ali had a lifelong allegiance to the Tan family. His loyalty was rewarded. Tan Chin Tuan employed him, sheltered him and pensioned him until the day he died, at the age of ninety.

To keep the peace between his estate's two fractious camps, the conflicts often required the services of the local law enforcers, with whom TCT soon became acquainted. The most memorable was John Dalley, the Chief of Police in Johore. A spontaneous and enthusiastic Irish daredevil who would plunge into a situation disregarding any danger to himself, Dalley was unconventional and a bit of a rebel, well suited to the unpredictable Malayan territory he patrolled. Later, during the war, as the Japanese sneaked down the Malayan coast towards Singapore, Colonel Dalley would become a legend in the defence of Malaya, leading an unpredictable band of rebel warriors nicknamed Dalforce. Later still, when the war was over, Dalley distinguished himself as the head of the Malayan Security Service.

TCT and Dalley became good friends and the Chief of Police permitted the banker to carry a gun on his visits to Johore. Dalley not only assisted TCT, but also helped his acquaintances. On one occasion, Tan Chin Tuan complained to Dalley on behalf of a friend who was having problems with violence on his own rubber estate in Johore. Without a moment's hesitation, the police chief and two of his constables arrested the troublemaker, a man named Ger Chai. Dalley recommended to the authorities that he be banished to China, which was the most dreaded penalty the British could levy on the criminal class at the time.

Soon after, two women arrived unannounced at Tan Chin Tuan's house. Weeping, one threw herself before TCT, beseeching him to save her husband, Ger Chai. Touched by her distress, he went to Dalley and asked if the man could be released. Dalley reacted like an awakened volcano. "First, you asked me to arrest him and now you want me to release him! I don't understand you," he erupted. Calming down, he agreed, on the condition TCT would stand surety for Ger Chai to the sum of $1,000, which represented a small fortune in those days.

When Ger Chai and his wife visited Tan Chin Tuan's home to thank him, the man literally fell to his knees with gratitude. TCT's sympathetic nature joined with his natural business acumen, and he hired the former rogue to handle security on the Kambau estate. Although a small man, Ger Chai walked with a confident swagger. He was an expert in the martial art of kung fu and, on more than one occasion, defended TCT, fighting three or four surly workers, armed only with his stick. With a flick of the wrists and a flash of stick, the attackers would be moaning and rolling on the ground. A loyal and effective employee, Ger Chai was lost during the Japanese occupation. TCT tried to trace him, to no avail.

Another memorable member of the Kambau estate was Lim Teck Swee, who excelled in the understanding of wild animals. On one occasion, TCT and Lim were walking with the workers when a tiger suddenly appeared on the path. TCT immediately took aim with his gun, but Lim snatched the gun away. Grabbing his umbrella, he quickly opened and closed it several times. To the amazement of all, the tiger fled, frightened by the benign weapon. Lim turned to his young employer and explained the importance of assessing risk in life. He cautioned, "You must learn to distinguish the ferocious from the harmless, and good tigers from bad."

"Good" tigers feared man. "Bad" tigers attacked. When a man-eating tiger had taken a man from the village, Lim organised a search party. He insisted upon walking in front; a tiger in possession of human prey was dangerous. The group followed the trail until they saw evidence of a man having been dragged into the swamp. Lim quickly produced several powerful firecrackers, throwing them into the jungle swamp. As he hurled the flashing thundersticks, Lim stepped backwards, in anticipation of a tiger attack. But the explosions had the desired effect; the tiger was frightened away, allowing the party to retrieve the body of the man.

Lim declared he would kill the tiger within three days. He built a hideout in the great cat's territory and waited. Using a puppy as live bait, he lured the tiger to the trap and shot it. Lim was the nearest thing to a gamekeeper that an estate devoted to rubber could appropriately employ. TCT paid him a salary, plus all the desired game he hunted. The meat was retailed in the village and a percentage of the proceeds presented to Lim. The meat from the wild boar was worth considerably more than the wages that Lim was paid each month. For Tan Chin Tuan, it was a pleasure employing such a talented man, who not only provided the plantation with food and profit, but a considerable amount of excitement.

These adventures were dramatic diversions in the serious business of estate management. Tan Chin Tuan was so skilful at it that most of the estates repossessed and maintained by Eastern Realty incurred minimal cost. He engaged and supervised literally hundreds of employees throughout Malaya and Singapore, waiting for the market to recover, so the bank could sell the properties at a profit. But witnessing the personal tragedies of people defeated by severe inflation intensified his already compassionate nature.

TCT also constructed houses on behalf of the bank. The work presented continuing challenges. For example, during the construction of fifty-two houses in Singapore's Kim Seng Road, it was discovered that the land was so swampy it required piles driven twenty feet into the ground. However, once built, the rental units were so popular that potential applicants had to draw lots to secure them. The project produced a 20 to 25 per cent profit for OCBC.

As a licensed property valuer, he attended auctions, looking for bargains for Eastern Realty. But his skill for knowing the true worth of a property soon became a disadvantage. People began to watch him, to see if he was bidding. He was forced to develop an intricate series of secret clues, which he strategically changed with each new auction. "If I take off my spectacles, I am making a bid," he would tell the auctioneer. Or "When I take out my pen and it points upwards, this is my signal to buy." He would scratch his ears, make unusual hand movements, remove his glasses and take out his handkerchief, using any means to disguise his interest in a property.

Occasionally, he would use this strategy in reverse, by openly demonstrating his interest. A friend of his could not obtain his reserve price for his seafront home because prices were falling. A year or so later, TCT suggested the time was now right to put the house up for auction again. Without his friend's knowledge, TCT attended the sale to make sure that bidders did not gang up to depress the price, counteracting their tactics with his own. An excited murmur went through the crowd — the manager of Eastern Realty was bidding! His participation created renewed competition for the property, so that his friend got the true value for his home, instead of being forced by auction gangs to sell at a pittance.

At another auction, Yeap Chor Ee, one of Penang's richest men and the owner of a private bank, began bidding for a property owned by Eastern Realty. TCT watched quietly from the corner. Using his covert gestures, he bid against the wealthy Malayan, raising the price of the property by 40 per cent of the fixed reserve. When Yeap learned that TCT had been the competing bidder, he came to see him, angry at first that he had paid a premium for the property. However, as a banker himself, Yeap, on reflection, appreciated Tan Chin Tuan's efforts to benefit OCBC. The two men became friends, with Yeap presenting TCT with a basket of rambutans every time he visited Singapore.

Yeap respected Tan Chin Tuan's staunch loyalty to the bank. OCBC also recognised this unwavering dedication. His boyhood association with his father's friends also proved advantageous to his career. In 1934, the bank chose him to represent them in their dealings with Singapore's most important and intimidating businessman — Tan Kah Kee.

Tan Kah Kee was the powerful and influential leader of Singapore's Chinese community during the first half of the twentieth century. Described, at his peak, as "the Henry Ford of Malaya", his inventiveness and daring made him one of the bank's best customers. Although the rubber planters, traders and manufacturers endured immense economic problems during the depression of the 1930s, their plight was insignificant compared to that of Tan Kah Kee's. He had been borrowing heavily to expand his rubber manufacturing plants and retail network, when the price of rubber suddenly crashed. From $1.14 per pound in 1925 to 35 cents per pound in 1929, it finally collapsed to a disastrous record low of just over 4 cents per pound in 1932. Stiff Japanese competition, particularly in the manufacturing of rubber shoes, worsened the situation. Tan Kah Kee was forced to sell shoes he had charged $1 a pair for in 1928, for 20 cents a pair four years later.

Tan Kah Kee's problems became the banks' problems. When OCBC was created, one major concern was the enormous loans given to the businessman by the predecessor banks. The OCBC and the British banks (which were also Tan's creditors) jointly acted to convert Tan Kah Kee & Co, an unlimited company, into a private limited liability company. Tan Kah Kee was named managing director, but the banks were determined to run his company for him by appointing directors to his board. He had little choice. OCBC vice-chairman Lee Kong Chian and joint managing director Yap Twee were made directors in Tan Kah Kee & Co Ltd. For Lee Kong Chian, it was a particularly awkward predicament, since Tan Kah Kee was his father-in-law. As Yap also felt uneasy about serving as a director, the two men pleaded that they could not be spared due to their senior positions at the bank. They searched for a comparatively junior yet suitable substitute to send as their deputy to confer with Tan Kah Kee. They selected Tan Chin Tuan.

TCT accepted the assignment to be the OCBC's representative with mixed feelings. He felt honoured, yet apprehensive. Tan Kah Kee was held in great awe and respect by all Chinese. He led an exemplary, disciplined, industrious and simple life. He was revered for his tireless devotion to Chinese education, but few felt comfortable in his formidable presence.

Yet Tan Kah Kee had been kind and cordial to the young boy who had accompanied his father to the Ee Hoe Hean club. He treated Tan Chin Tuan gently, like a favourite nephew. TCT became the sympathetic listener he needed and almost the only one who could speak with him productively. His success in representing the OCBC led the Hongkong and Shanghai Bank, and the Chartered Bank, to also use him as their link. Distressingly, the message TCT was asked to convey was the banks' intentions to liquidate the assets of Tan Kah Kee & Co Ltd.

Although his business empire was decimated by April 1934, Tan Kah Kee's economic demise did little damage to his standing as a social and political lion. By being close to and accepted by the lion in distress, TCT gained substantial respect within the Chinese community.

Tan Chin Tuan's association with Tan Kah Kee continued beyond the boardroom. In 1937, Japan expanded its invasion of China. Now, the face of war had a deeply personal connection to the residents of the Lion City. Singapore's Chinese population, many of whom were immigrants from the mainland, was devastated by the news. They wished to help and sought a leader. Tan Kah Kee was the only man who could rally the community.

The news of the Japanese assault affected the various groups that made up the Chinese community in Singapore in different ways. The Kuomintang, or Nationalist Party of China (which had a chapter in Singapore), hoped to acquire more support. The Malayan Communist Party also saw the incursion as a way of gaining support. The locally born and bred Chinese were emotionally involved with the conflict too. Although the Straits Chinese were loyal British subjects, they could not ignore the anguished cry from the land of their ancestors and the wellspring of their race and culture. They considered the Japanese attack immoral, and as the tales of violence and cruelty unfolded, the Chinese in Singapore were tormented with rage and a sense of impotence.

Tan Kah Kee provided an alternate and more comfortable rallying point. He was neither a member of the Kuomintang (although he supported Chiang Kai-shek) nor the Communists (though he saw much to admire in Mao Zedong after the Long March). He also had the support of the British during this volatile period, who considered his position the most palatable.

Tan Kah Kee completely dedicated himself to this cause, wielding a power and influence as no Chinese leader in the region had done before. He not only became a hero to the people but also secured his place in history. Tan Kah Kee's singular passion united all Chinese, both elite and impoverished.

The Singapore China Relief Fund Committee (SCFRC), a movement to raise funds to support China's wartime distress, began with the residents of Singapore and Malaya and rapidly spread across China's supporters and Chinese-born immigrants. Tan Kah Kee was elected its chairman, and its headquarters were set up at the Ee Hoe Hean Club.

As the British were not at war with Japan, the Straits Chinese, as British subjects, had to be discreet about supporting the cause. Although Tan Chin Tuan withheld his support for the anti-Japanese movements, he was willing to join the SCRFC, as its only mandate was fund-raising. Every possible avenue of entertainment and recreation was approached for money, from the concert hall to the theatre and opera house, dance hall, sports stadium, fun fair and carnival site. TCT and his wife, Helene, were prominent advocates of the SCRFC and OCBC served as its treasurer. One of the many initiatives their committee sponsored was a three-night concert at the Victoria Memorial Hall, featuring the popular Wuhan Choir. This troupe of thirty singers, from Wuhan, China, had performed throughout China, encouraging the population to save the country by resisting the enemy. In Singapore, the sincerity of the singers and their conductor, Xia Zhiqiu, inspired new donations.

Towkays of the Chinese Chamber of Commerce gave monthly,

workers contributed through payroll deductions, hawkers offered their takings, school children sold flags and flowers, and people threw their spare change into the ubiquitous collection boxes.

The European community tended towards benign ambivalence to the fund-raising, but occasionally unpleasant incidents occurred. One group of fundraisers solicited a British agency, Sime Darby, for a donation, but was dismissed abruptly amid racist epithets. The members of the group urged violent retaliation, but Tan Chin Tuan knew instinctively that such a move would reflect negatively on the movement. Instead, he counselled the offended members to quietly urge the Chinese community to boycott the agency's foremost product — a brand of cigarettes known as Black Cat. In short order, Sime Darby issued both an apology and a sizeable contribution. After that, the mere threat of being boycotted was a discreet but persuasive fund-raising incentive.

TCT found creative ways to raise money in the most unusual quarters. As the bank was temporarily not buying properties, he used, with the bank's knowledge and permission, his expertise as a licensed house valuer, to attend property auctions and privately purchase bargain houses for resale. On one occasion, at the auction of a house belonging to an Arab family, he offered the highest bid. Although he obtained the home fairly, the Chinese tenant who resided in the Amoy Street house was annoyed. He had hoped to buy it, but could not penetrate the intricate signals TCT used with the auctioneer.

The tenant complained to a friend, Yap Twee, a former managing director of OCBC, begging Yap to intervene and persuade Tan Chin Tuan to relinquish the house. TCT was caught between the unfairness of the request and his respect for Yap, for he could not allow Yap to lose face with his friend. He made the best of a bad situation, by setting the price for the home at 80 per cent of its estimated market value and demanding that the tenant donate the difference to the Singapore China Relief Fund Committee.

TCT's work for the SCRFC was satisfying. His admiration for Tan Kah Kee and sympathy with his mission might have been the original catalysts that spurred him into action, but once he began to achieve tangible results for the cause, he saw that his efforts could make a difference. This first significant foray into public life would not be his last. However, next time, the challenge would be even greater.

The merger of the three Hokkien banks into the Oversea-Chinese Banking Corporation had brought new faces to the board of directors, including a gentleman from one of the old moneyed families of Malacca. Chee Swee Cheng, who was appointed the first chairman of OCBC, was a philosopher, folklorist and historical narrator. His skills as a great conciliator and unifier were vital during the banks' amalgamation negotiations. As Chee had expertise in property and real estate, the new chairman took a particular interest in Tan Chin Tuan and his department, Eastern Realty. This association led to friendships with other influential Straits Chinese, who served as role models and taught him the subtleties of political interaction in a colonial state.

One mentor was Chan Sze Jin. History remembers him as S.J. Chan, a King's Scholar and Cambridge-educated lawyer who served as a member of the Legislative Council from 1927 to 1930 and the Executive Council from 1935 to 1940. Chan was humble, self-effacing and generous, untypical of most public figures. He was a founding member and the first president of the Island Club, which TCT had reluctantly joined at the urging of John Laycock, a barrister who consulted for the bank. The lawyer and the banker would become close friends.

Although Tan Chin Tuan preferred tennis and badminton, Laycock advised that he join the golf club. Initially, TCT privately considered golf a sport for old men. But he soon came to appreciate the game, the social life of the golf club and its influential members. In essence, the Island Club became a classroom in the education of a potential politician.

Several important members of the golf club were dedicated to improving conditions for the Chinese. One of Singapore's most experienced legislators, Tan Cheng Lock, fought for greater Chinese participation in the governance of the colony. He was a Malacca rubber tycoon, a founder of the Ho Hong Bank and one of the original directors of OCBC. President of the Straits Chinese British Association (SCBA), Tan Cheng Lock sat on the Legislative Council between 1923 and 1934 and on the Executive Council from 1933 to 1937. Another powerful citizen, Wee Swee Teow, also served on the Legislative Council between 1930-1933. Although private and unpretentious, he steadfastly defended public interests. Wee, S.J. Chan and Tan Cheng Lock were pressing the British for concessions, using the SCBA as their constituency. The three men urged Tan Chin Tuan to join their organisation and their struggle. Their commitment opened his eyes to the reality of the injustices entrenched in colonialism and the need for change.

One arena of overt racism was the civil service. In 1904, a new regulation limited entry into the service to "natural-born British subjects of pure European descent on both sides".

As early as 1923, Tan Cheng Lock had made a speech to the Legislative Council against the notorious "colour bar". S.J. Chan and Wee Swee Teow joined the attack and the SCBA wrote petitions.

The civil service issue was part of a broader campaign, which the Straits Chinese had been waging for some time. They sought to pressure the British to expand and underwrite education in the English language. They argued that English could serve as the common language of all citizens, citing economic utility in an international trading environment and political unity in a multiracial society. English could help foster a Malayan consciousness.

Higher education was another concern, which warranted continuous lobbying by the Straits Chinese. As far back as 1914, the Reverend J.S. Nagle, the principal of the Anglo-Chinese School, had initiated the concept of an Anglo-Chinese College. Tan Kah Kee supported the idea by donating $10,000, and TCT's father had contributed $3,000. An Anglo-Chinese College Council was formed, and Nagle sought the approval of the colonial government to produce the first arts and sciences higher education institute in Singapore and Malaya.

The British response was cool, and the proposed college was denied. The initiative, however, goaded the British into finally producing an educational plan, which in 1928 ultimately materialised as Raffles College. A few prominent Chinese felt bitter and left out of the British plans. But Tan Kah Kee, demonstrating his unwavering support for education, whether in English or Chinese, endowed $10,000. Raffles College came to be regarded as a British attempt to placate the English-speaking Straits Chinese, whose loyalty had become invaluable.

In another act of apparent political expediency, the British created three services for Asians, each one granted the prefix Straits Settlements — the Medical Service in 1932, the Civil Service in 1934 and the Legal Service in 1937.

These concessions by the British rulers finally allowed the Straits Chinese to advance both educationally and professionally, securing their foothold in the bureaucracy.

The successful efforts of players in the Straits Chinese British Association inspired Tan Chin Tuan to become more involved in civic duties. In 1939, he became a committee member of the Straits Settlements (Singapore) Association and joined the Singapore Branch (Chinese Section) of the Malayan Patriotic Fund, a fund-raising movement, which supported the British war effort. His growing prominence in the community positioned him for even more influence, which he would ultimately use to fight for the rights of his people against the abuses of colonialism.

Tan Chin Tuan now had the maturity, experience and social contacts to serve in the public arena. His mentor S.J. Chan had already served on the Executive Council and Legislative Council respectively. As these positions were unpaid, business obligations led to resignations, and despite the honour of a governmental nomination, there was a steady turnover in the ranks of unofficial members.

In 1939, several positions opened up on the twenty-five-member Board of Municipal Commissioners. In August, a letter unexpectedly arrived at TCT's seaside house at Pasir Panjang stating that, if he was willing, the Governor of the Straits Settlements had appointed him to serve on the Municipal Commission.

The commission managed Singapore's municipal matters. It comprised the commission president and twenty-five members, all appointed by the governor. For efficiency, the administration was divided into seven committees, with the president presiding *ex officio* at each committee meeting.

Tan Chin Tuan never discovered the identity of the person who recommended him for this prestigious nomination. It might have been his barrister friend John Laycock, himself a municipal commissioner earlier in the decade; or it might be due to the links he had formed with Tan Kah Kee, with the China-born OCBC directors and clients, or with the Straits Chinese legislators and the SCBA. As President of the Singapore Ratepayers Association, TCT often made representations to the government. In any case, his name had reached the ears of the officials. He accepted, with the blessings of the chairman and the managing director of the bank, who considered the appointment not only an honour, but excellent public relations.

TCT was barely thirty-one years old when he was appointed to the commission, probably the youngest representative ever. At first, his callowness showed. The European incumbents shredded his self-confidence, taunting him with jeers and insults the first time he attempted to make a speech. They sneered, particularly on matters where they were solidly grounded, and he was exposed as a novice. After this initial savaging, TCT dared not open his mouth for another six months. It was a brutal way to learn a lesson, but thereafter, when he did speak, he did so prepared, informed and with authority.

Although the Europeans showed him little mercy in the political arena, they were curiously friendly and warm in any business context. As an assistant exchange manager, Tan Chin Tuan had to deal with exchange brokers such as E.A. Brown, one of the old guard on the commission. Relentlessly ferocious in the municipal chambers, Brown was courteous and pleasant on TCT's turf in the banking hall.

Colonial Singapore was the pinnacle of British superiority and aloofness. As modern amenities made the East more accessible and liveable to the British, families replaced individuals stationed in the colony. Inevitably, as more British households were set up, a way of life was established, according to its rigid upper middle class standards, replete with its social obligations, rituals and taboos. The presence of British women was the vital force in this gregarious lifestyle. But they held inflexible attitudes towards gender and class, causing their menfolk to become more conscious of ethnic and class distinctions, and more conservative and withdrawn in their relations with Asians than in the days of the mostly male British society.

Municipal president William Bartley personified the condescending face of colonialism. Eight years in office had sharpened his arrogance and confidence. Bartley demanded subservience from the Asians on the commission. Racism of any kind was upsetting to Tan Chin Tuan. It was a cause he would champion his entire life.

Two months into TCT's appointment, Bartley retired. Had he not done so, Tan Chin Tuan would likely have resigned himself at the end of his term. Yet, in his own way, Bartley was a visionary. On his departure, he spoke of his desire for a city of the future, with parks and open spaces, a dynamic civic centre with magnificent public buildings, a modernised business district and a variety of attractive residential areas. Without knowing it, he was describing the impressive and prosperous Singapore of the late twentieth century.

Bartley was gone, but his disdain had infected the commission. The old guard sought to intimidate Bartley's successor, Lazarus Rayman. Rayman was an experienced Malayan Civil Service grade one A officer, who had been a treasurer, under-secretary and acting financial secretary. At their monthly meeting, the European commissioners encircled the new municipal president. E.A. Brown warned Rayman to expect to be "dissected" after the honeymoon period. The threat was in the open. Rayman could not expect the whole-hearted co-operation of the commission.

During Bartley's tenure, some improvements had been made to the city. The civic centre had three large, new, public buildings — The Supreme Court, the Municipal Offices (now City Hall) and the Fullerton Building. Electricity was supplied by a power station built by the municipality in 1927, the St. James Power Station, which was able to produce 22,000 kilowatts by 1929.

These edifices stood in stark contrast to the wretched tenement housing of the masses. In the densely populated area to the south and across the river from the civic centre, rows of houses were divided into tiny cubicles, into which whole families were crammed. The Municipal Ordinance had traditionally turned a blind eye to the landlords who profited from the overcrowding of these unfit dwellings.

The Singapore Rayman inherited was tarnished by this urban congestion. He considered it his greatest challenge and longed to tackle the problem, but international concerns began to eclipse local matters. At his first meeting with the commissioners, Rayman advised: "The Empire is at war with Germany." Although the war in Europe did not yet directly affect Singapore, preparations had to be made.

Tan Chin Tuan's respect for Rayman increased as they worked together. Although dignified, the unorthodox president was not pretentious. As an Ashkenasi Jew, he understood suffering and racism. He and TCT could discuss ideas intellectually without friction. In fact, the more the two men debated, the closer they became. Rayman tested his young protégé by setting him tasks and upon their successful completion, assigning more. He also began to use Tan Chin Tuan to present his views to the other members of the commission.

This new association brought TCT increased authority and prestige. His initial assignments were not overly demanding. The commission was divided into committees. TCT was appointed to the same committees that his predecessor, Ng Sen Choy, a tailor who owned the Wing Loong company in High Street, had sat on.

Tan Chin Tuan did not expect these appointments to be much of a challenge. Committee Six, concerned with parks and gardens, met only four times a year. Committee One dealt with the Registry of Vehicles.

From the beginning, TCT clashed with Major Ross, the Registrar of Vehicles. One of the registrar's responsibilities was to issue licences to the operators of every form of vehicular transport using the roads. Another was to sit as a quasi-magistrate, trying traffic offences. Officious and haughty, the bureaucrat held court, ruling not only on wealthier car owners, but on the impoverished ordinary citizens, such as syces, taxi drivers, busmen, lorry drivers and rickshaw pullers. The lower their station, the more Ross would scold, even as he fined them. The power, which he loved to exercise, had gone to his head.

Ross attended the Committee One meetings as if he was holding court, interrupting incessantly. Occasionally, TCT brought a case forward for discussion, but the discourteous registrar refused to listen or respond. Although Ross' bullying offended Tan Chin Tuan's sense of fairness, he endured more than a year of frustration. Finally, the time seemed right to retaliate. During one session, he posed a seemingly innocent question to the municipal president.

"Sir," he asked politely, "will you please enlighten me as to whether the Registrar of Vehicles is in attendance as an adviser or as a member?"

Rayman, who had not anticipated such a question, cautiously

replied, "He is an adviser. Obviously he is not a member."

TCT pressed on: "As an adviser, has he any right of speech?"

As expected, Ross protested that he indeed did have this prerogative, but Tan Chin Tuan had the answer he needed. He turned to the four other commissioners, insisting "as an adviser, he should only speak when his advice is asked".

The registrar exploded and the assembly erupted. Rayman attempted to smooth over the furore, promising to reflect on the ruling. Later, Rayman asked TCT why he had asked the question. "I just want to make it clear," replied Tan Chin Tuan. "If I think I'm right, I'll fight."

Much to the registrar's annoyance, Rayman declared at the next meeting that TCT was correct. "He is an adviser and as such he cannot speak until asked." From then on, whenever Ross forgot himself and interrupted, Tan Chin Tuan would ask the chairman to remind the registrar he was there in the capacity of an adviser. With skilful wit, TCT had muzzled the man.

This wrong was one of many hundreds that TCT would act to right, regardless of the size of the odds or the strength of the opponent, for the pure purpose of justice. He lived by a phrase of his own making, "Fight for right. Fear not might."

Rayman rewarded TCT's successful handling of the officious bureaucrat by assigning him to the coveted Committee Four, which controlled public works. Its mandate included overseeing the municipal architects and engineers, and supervising the low-cost housing pro-gramme of the Singapore Improvement Trust. Using the expertise he had developed with Eastern Realty, Tan Chin Tuan impressed Rayman further.

Having proven himself ready, Rayman appointed TCT to the most important committee in the Municipal Commission, the Finance Committee. This committee represented the municipality in its disputes with the government, particularly over the question of funding. Working long hours together, the municipal president prepared TCT with the facts and arguments to support their position. In these meetings, Tan Chin Tuan and Rayman would confront the government's side, led by the financial secretary and the impressively titled senior unofficial member of the legislature, the imposing Sir John Bagnall. Sir John was also the chairman of Straits Trading Company and the connection between this important position and his status as senior unofficial was a respected convention of that period.

There was a certain parallel in this situation, for, not too many years later, Tan Chin Tuan would become chairman of Straits Trading Company, and he too would be awarded the distinction of senior unofficial member of the Legislature. The experience TCT gained on the committees would be invaluable in subsequent years.

But for now, the shadow of war was lengthening, and he was about to embark upon a journey requiring great courage and sacrifice. His loyalty to the bank would put his life at risk.

War

The fear of war stalked the island of Singapore like a menacing shadow. Japan had formed an Axis with Germany and Italy. Europe was fighting for its life, and Britain was preoccupied with battles closer to home. Each day, as the war escalated throughout Europe and North Africa, the once inconceivable possibility of invasion inched closer to reality.

Historically, the British considered it both their duty and prerogative to defend their colonial outposts and naval bases. But mistakenly believing "Fortress Singapore" to be impenetrable, they were more complacent than in other regions.

The British refused to seek the help of the dominant Chinese. Although there was an established volunteer army, the Straits Settlements Volunteer Force (SSVF), the recruits were not permitted to carry arms. They were only invited to demonstrate their prowess during pageants, ceremonies and peacetime shooting competitions. The British Government had no intention to deploy them — in fact, their training and weapons were inadequate for real action.

Instead, the British assembled a motley combined force of British, Indian and Australian troops. Not until the disastrous final moments before the Japanese invasion were the Chinese permitted to play a part in the defence of their adopted home, when the courageous Colonel John Dalley (the former Chief of Police in Johore) of the Federated Malay States police force, assembled his defiant guerrillas.

Two years earlier, Dalley had proposed such a scheme to the government, but nobody listened to "the mad Irishman". He later told Tan Chin Tuan that had he been given six months notice or even three months, it would have satisfied him, instead of this last minute request. Still, he did his best and led the hundreds of Chinese volunteers who flocked to join his Dalforce in a gallant, if doomed, attempt to resist the Japanese 25th Army.

Dalley recruited his men from all classes of Chinese society and all shades of political opinion. This divergent assembly included the locally born, English-educated Singapore Volunteer Forces, the Chinese nationalist Kuomintang Youth Group and the Communist Public Armed Forces.

Colonel Dalley survived the war and became the head of the Malayan Security Service in post-war Malaya, but he left his mark on Singapore's history. The exploits of Dalforce, or Dalcompany, or Dalley's Desperadoes, will always be remembered.

The government in pre-war Singapore used the Chinese in a civilian role. They served in Passive Defence (later called Civil Defence) that included ambulance driving, stretcher bearing, first-aid assistance, nursing and air raid precaution. Generally, most of the Passive Defence volunteers were English-educated. The China-born and Chinese-educated were more physically active, and became an indispensable, rugged labour force assisting the government and the military, naval and air services. Humble and stoic, these heroes allowed themselves to be mobilised as coolies.

Anticipating an imminent invasion, the government asked Singapore's municipal commission to nominate two members to the Passive Defence Council. Rayman and Tan Chin Tuan were appointed to the posts. Despite his responsibilities to the bank, TCT considered this important assignment his duty, both to the commission president and to the colony.

The chairman of the Passive Defence Council was the colonial secretary S W. Jones, the second-highest ranking government official in Singapore. Jones would later play a pivotal role relating to Britain's interest in TCT during the war. Tan Chin Tuan was invited to draft the Passive Defence regulations alongside another important council member, Kenneth K. O'Connor. A barrister and partner in the firm of Drew and Napier, he was intelligent, stimulating and congenial. O'Connor and TCT would meet in the evening at O'Connor's house and often worked into the early hours of the morning.

O'Connor's many contributions, which included formulating the post-war Debtor-Creditor Ordinance, resulted in his being appointed Attorney-General after the war and rewarded with a knighthood.

As the situation worsened, the Commander-in-Chief, Far East, Air Chief Marshal Sir Robert Brooke-Popham, conducted a briefing, warning that although Britain would defend Singapore and send forces if necessary, the country must be prepared for bombing. The municipality must ensure that the strategically vital utilities, such as the waterworks and electrical power plants, would still be operational in the event of attack, as their continuance would be crucial during any conflict.

At a municipal council meeting, the engineers of the St. James Power Station at Pasir Panjang made a presentation. They estimated that they required spare parts for 50 per cent of the twelve-year-old plant to avoid a disruption of service. TCT could not understand how, logically, 50 per cent of spare parts would suffice in the event of a direct hit by aerial attack. The plant's chief engineer agreed. "Actually, we cannot be completely covered unless we have 100 per cent of all parts in store." At the idea of assembling 100 per cent of the parts, TCT retorted, tongue in cheek, "Then we might as well build another station somewhere else."

Later, at a meeting of the Passive Defence Council, another military officer, Brigadier Ivan Simson, the Chief Engineer of Malaya Command, was advised of the engineer's recommendation for 50 per cent of spare parts. "If that's what they need, then order the parts."

Again, TCT suggested that half would not ensure complete protection and that only 100 per cent of spare parts would be an effective safeguard. Brigadier Simson was convinced and agreed. "Then order 100 per cent of parts."

TCT quietly repeated his comment. "Surely, it is preferable to build another station at another site," he smiled. Amused by this response, the councillors laughed. Then they grew thoughtful. TCT had used humour to focus debate on a difficult decision. One by one they recognised the absurdity of the logic and the seriousness of the dilemma.

Tan Chin Tuan's leadership qualities quickly earned him the respect of his peers. As he gained in stature and self-confidence, he became increasingly outspoken on the subject of racial discrimination. His words gained more currency as he earned acceptance from his British colleagues.

Racism seeped through every layer of the hierarchy of Passive Defence, just as it did in every other aspect of Singapore's colonial existence. Local men were destined to be subordinate. TCT took his complaint to the government, demanding that the Chinese also be given senior posts. The government responded by appointing him to a senior position — Divisional Commander of Air Raid Precaution, responsible for recruiting men as air raid wardens and supervising the building of air raid shelters.

His recruitment drive succeeded, supported by his influence in the Tan Clan and his connections with Tan Kah Kee. But this new responsibility, plus his numerous other civil defence duties on the Passive Defence Council and his commitment to the bank, meant TCT worked long, draining days and equally long nights.

Such dedication took its toll. He was exhausting himself. Concerned,

TCT's doctor demanded he rest. But mindful of his banking duties, Tan Chin Tuan used a brief holiday as an opportunity to explore OCBC's alternatives in the event of war. In September 1941, with war looming, he and his wife, Helene, travelled to Australia. During these uncertain times a government letter, accrediting TCT as a member of the Passive Defence Council — an essential service — protected them. Should there be any emergencies, he could return to Singapore on priority air passage.

The journey to Sydney took four days. The Tans caught a flying boat from Singapore to Surabaya in Indonesia. It took another day to fly to Darwin in Australia. The following day, the travellers boarded an aircraft to Townsville and finally onward to Sydney.

Australia was known for its whites-only immigration policy. As this was TCT's first trip to an all-white nation, he was apprehensive about the kind of reception he and Helene might receive. Fortunately, their entry visas had been secured by OCBC's principal Australian agent, the Bank of New South Wales (later to become Westpac), so the Australian bank had paved the way.

The Australians could not have been more welcoming. The customs officers at the first port of call, Darwin, treated the Tans respectfully. Later, when they missed dinner at the hotel, the manager offered complimentary chicken sandwiches to satisfy their hunger. In Townsville, after a meal of roast pork, the hotel manager inquired if his guests enjoyed their meal. Hearing it was rated delicious, he proudly credited the hotel's excellent cuisine to his Chinese cook.

These pleasant encounters diminished any fear of intolerance. Consequently, TCT was less prepared when he encountered the first incident of entrenched prejudice among the Australian officials. When he arrived in Sydney, he was instructed to report to immigration headquarters. He did so, accompanied by Harold Brown, the manager of the travel department of the Bank of New South Wales. The immigration officer at the duty counter demanded that Tan Chin Tuan surrender his passport. Without a glance at its owner, he issued TCT a receipt, which, he mumbled, would redeem the document when the visitor was ready to leave the country.

TCT protested. He asked why passports, issued in Singapore to British subjects of Caucasian origin, were not withheld? Why was the Australian government making an example of Chinese British subjects? Embarrassed by the insensitive treatment of his guest, Harold Brown implored the authorities to reconsider, stating categorically that the Bank of New South Wales would vouch for this banker from Singapore. His pleas were likewise ignored.

Numbed by this injustice, a disillusioned Tan Chin Tuan continued his journey, travelling southwards to Canberra. The Bank of New South Wales had arranged luxurious accommodation at the Hotel Canberra opposite Parliament House. TCT was grateful for the bank's help, as he probably could not have secured rooms in this prestigious hotel without the assistance of Australia's largest financial institution.

Parliament was in session and the hotel dining room overflowed with cabinet ministers and senior members of the government. The waiter took pride in identifying these illustrious diners to his other guests. One evening, he pointed to an elegant man with white hair. "That is Senator Collins, the minister of foreign affairs. The tall man with him is John Curtin, our prime minister."

Whether the Australian prime minister was a man of rare intelligent curiosity, an intuitive diplomat, or whether someone whispered that a prominent banker from Singapore was registered at the hotel, will never be known. But as the Tans were sipping their coffee after an elegant meal, TCT looked up to see the prime minister standing beside his table. After introducing himself and exchanging the usual pleasantries, Curtin asked if they were enjoying their holiday. He caught the slight hesitation in TCT's polite affirmative answer. He asked if anything was wrong. Tan Chin Tuan revealed his discomfort concerning the impounding of his and his wife's passports. Curtin placed his hand on TCT's shoulder. "Don't allow that to upset you," he urged. "Continue your travels and keep on enjoying yourself." These were not hollow words or comforting phrases as TCT would soon discover.

Arriving in Melbourne, the Tans heard the horrifying news. On December 7, the Japanese onslaught had begun: Pearl Harbor had been bombed, and Hong Kong and the Philippines invaded. The Japanese simultaneously landed forces in southern Thailand and Kota Bahru in northern Malaya. The Malayan airfield had fallen by evening. The Japanese 25th army, comprising the 5th, 18th and Imperial Guards divisions, began to overrun Malaya.

Back in Singapore, Lieutenant General Arthur E. Percival commanded 80,000 troops, but despite his requests for two tank brigades, he still had no tanks. The impotent fixed gun emplacements faced out to sea, and the 158 aircraft were inferior. Their only defence depended on the two great British battleships, the *Prince of Wales* and the *Repulse*, now anchored in the harbour.

Just before dawn, on December 8, 1941, the first Japanese bombs fell on Singapore. Seventeen planes, originating in Indochina, attacked Raffles Place and the Seletar and Tengah airfields. Sixty people were killed and 700 injured.

Confidently, the Japanese began their advance down the Malay Peninsula, while the unprepared Allied forces retreated.

Without air cover, the battleships were defenceless. Japanese torpedo bombers sank the *Prince of Wales* and the *Repulse* on December 10, in an engagement off the east coast of Malaya. The Commander-in-Chief of the Eastern Fleet, Sir Thomas Philips, and more than 800 of his fighting men, went down with the warships.

Having conquered the air, the Japanese had mastered the sea. Two days later, a state of emergency was declared. Singapore was militarily isolated and helpless.

Anxious over the myriad uncertainties caused by the outbreak of war, Tan Chin Tuan and Helene caught the first available train from Melbourne to Sydney, to arrange their air passage home.

An urgent message was waiting for them at the hotel in Sydney from Harold Brown of the Bank of New South Wales. "The immigration department has been asking when you would be back. They are most anxious to see you."

The following day, Brown accompanied TCT to immigration headquarters and both were ushered into the office of the chief. He seemed petulant. "I believe you have been complaining to the prime minister." To Tan Chin Tuan's surprise and silent delight, the chief of immigration stated that the prime minister had personally intervened and asked what law or regulation sanctioned the retention of the passports. He searched TCT's face for an answer. Receiving none, he continued, "If there ever was a statute, I can't find it. Now I'm in trouble."

The chief then begged Tan Chin Tuan to accept his apology. Obviously, he had been told to do so by the minister responsible for immigration, who had incurred the wrath of Prime Minister Curtin. In order to prove to his superiors that he had indeed made amends to TCT, the chief then put pen to paper and composed an elaborate admission of guilt. Signing it, he pushed it meekly across the desk. TCT read it and took out his pen. "I accept your apology," he wrote above his signature.

The serendipitous meeting with John Curtin benefited others who had been subjected to the same treatment. By speaking up for his rights, Tan Chin Tuan stopped Australia's practice of retaining Asian passports. A week or two later, the Australian High Commission in Singapore informed TCT that the invidious practice of retaining passports on the basis of race had been discarded. The letter went on to explain that, in fact, there had never been a formal regulation, but an entrenched practice, initially introduced to keep track of the Chinese gold prospectors who had a habit of disappearing into the countryside.

TCT found this ironic. "They did not know that this Chinese would never run away."

TCT and Helene returned to Singapore on a reliable but uncomfortable Dakota, which had to refuel twice before setting out from Darwin, flying low to avoid Japanese fighters. Once home, Tan Chin Tuan took immediate steps to send Helene and their son and two daughters back to Australia, to the relative safety of Sydney. With his family protected, he again turned his attention to the bank and his public service.

TCT now invested all his time in the war effort. As Divisional Commander of Air Raid Precaution, he wore a brown tin hat with a white stripe in the front, which entitled him to go anywhere when the air raid sirens sounded, despite the curfews and restrictions. This exemption was a privilege for an Asian and proof he had established his trustworthiness with the British.

Air Raid Precaution had to ensure there was no repetition of the disastrous initial air attack upon Singapore: the first Japanese bombers had used the bright lights of the homes and street lamps as their beacon. With their command of the skies virtually unchallenged, the Japanese raiders continued their assault on Singapore. TCT made sure the blackout order was rigidly observed. Throughout the bombing, the Japanese studiously ignored the St. James Power Station, knowing that before long they would need the electrical power for themselves.

Tan Chin Tuan was also responsible for supervising the air raid drills and the construction of shelters. The government had decided, for the safety of the community, not to concentrate its citizens in huge public shelters, but to disperse the population to camps outside the town. Those who remained within the congested city were encouraged to tunnel into the hillsides and dig trenches in any open space.

The Japanese advance from Kota Bahru to Singapore's eventual surrender took seventy days. As the enemy drew nearer, it was extraordinarily difficult to maintain a semblance of order. The continuous rumble of explosions, the tension of surprise bombing raids and the continuous pounding of mortar shells were too much for the faint hearted. The government watched its public works department eroding, as men simply bolted in fear. The Singapore Harbour Board was also left stranded by terrified men, whose compulsion for personal safety overcame their spirit of public duty.

The lack of manpower had reached crisis proportions. Desperate for help, the governor, Sir Thomas Shenton Whitelegge Thomas, appealed to Tan Kah Kee. Only he had the personal authority to organise the Chinese labourers. It took several attempts before Tan Kah Kee relented. He was exhausted by the earlier China Relief campaigning and by the toll of the Japanese attacks.

On December 30, 1941, Tan Kah Kee formed the Singapore Chinese Mobilisation Council. Under his command, 3,000 Chinese men arrived daily to perform a variety of essential tasks, from clearing debris at bomb sites to digging trenches. The men worked tirelessly at the naval base, the airfields and on the battle lines. They repaired roads, carried supplies and were the only available source of coolie labour. They loyally served a beloved patriarch, whose example of personal sacrifice moved them to volunteer.

One particular incident demonstrated the profound respect these men had for Tan Kah Kee. The Colonial Financial Secretary, H. Weisberg, asked Tan Chin Tuan to personally supervise the burning of all unused currency notes, so they would not fall into the hands of the enemy. TCT met with Tan Kah Kee, to arrange for labourers to fulfil this assignment. Tan Kah Kee summoned his closest aides, Lau Boh Tan and Ng Aik Huan. He bestowed an honour on TCT when he said, "*Chin Tuan hiah kong*" (Elder brother Chin Tuan says) before explaining the mission. There was no higher compliment than to be called "elder brother" by the great Tan Kah Kee.

The following morning, at the request of Tan Kah Kee, twenty men in two large lorries met Tan Chin Tuan outside the China Building. "You know, this is dangerous work," TCT cautioned them. "There may be bombing where we are going." Without reservation or pause, they replied as if in unison: "*Kah Kee Peh* (Uncle Kah Kee) told us to do this. Therefore even if we were to die we would be happy."

The purpose of this secret operation was to destroy whatever could not be removed, denying it to the enemy. The intention was to burn the banknotes. OCBC, the Hong Kong and Shanghai Bank and other British banks pooled their inventory of high denomination Straits banknotes, adding them to the currency held by the government. An officer from the treasury department dutifully copied down the serial numbers of the notes. One of the world's most expensive bonfires was lit and each bank credited with the amount it consigned to the flames.

Death is the tragic but inevitable by-product of war. Haunted by the potential fate of these brave men, TCT felt compelled to arrange for the evacuation of those Chinese whose activities had placed them in jeopardy. The Japanese had already inflicted barbaric reprisals upon the citizens of China, particularly in Nanking. In Singapore, the Chinese who held the same anti-Japanese position risked similar brutality. Yet no plans had been made to protect them. The governor, Sir Shenton Thomas, was as resolutely non-committal on this issue as he was on everything else during these dire times. Even the Europeans were forced to make vital decisions in a vacuum. Worried about the safety of their loved ones, most Europeans sent their families away. But the indecisive governor demonstrated no leadership regarding any civilian evacuation.

Later, as the end drew near, there was a selective withdrawal of European men, ships and aeroplanes from their bases in Singapore to the Dutch East Indies. Yet even as this was happening, neither official word nor official help was ever extended to the Chinese. The reverse was true, as a number of Chinese who wished to leave were coldly refused exit permits.

Angered by this inhumanity, Tan Chin Tuan protested to the government. Typically, when TCT complained of an injustice, he was given the responsibility of amending the situation, as he was in this instance. He instituted an evacuation registry on the fourth floor of the China Building, the same building that housed the OCBC. As it was impractical to attempt the relocation of large numbers of Chinese, he concentrated his efforts on those brave men and their families who were marked for reprisal.

Tan Chin Tuan was alarmed to discover that there was no official initiative to protect and evacuate Tan Kah Kee. The same governor who had six weeks earlier begged this great man to take a leading role in the war effort had now apparently forgotten him. This was inconceivable and inexcusable — Tan Kah Kee's prominence and efforts on behalf of the Chinese made him an enemy of Japan. He would be the first to be hunted down.

On January 11, 1942, Kuala Lumpur in Malaya fell. By January 25, central Johore was taken. Now, nothing stood between the Japanese and the causeway connecting Malaya with Singapore. On January 30, 1942, two weeks before the British military surrendered to the Japanese, a delegation accompanied Tan Kah Kee to the governor's mansion. It included aides Lau Boh Tan and Ng Aik Huan, Yap Geok Twee and Tan Chin Tuan. Shenton Thomas' curt response gave Tan Kah Kee the answer he needed.

In a futile attempt to slow the Japanese incursion, the British blew up a section of the causeway and ten oil storage tanks at the naval base in Sembawang. Black smoke filled the sky, producing a grim and grimy foreboding. Within four days, the Japanese troops had repaired the damage. In the early hours of February 3, Tan Kah Kee and his party left in two motor launches for Sumatra. He spent some time there and then travelled to Java, circulating between Malang, Batu and other towns throughout the war to avoid detection.

Tan Chin Tuan, also a marked man at the hands of the Japanese, would depart the following day. But his reasons for leaving were different and he did so reluctantly.

TCT was forced to leave Singapore at the request of his employers. The directors of OCBC had taken certain steps to protect the bank in the event of a Japanese occupation. For some time, the bank had been watching the growing conflict in the Far East and was preparing for the worst. Loans had been reduced and funds deployed to improve reserves and liquidity. All transferable assets, such as deposits, credit balances and gilt-edged securities, had already been dispatched to Britain, converted into pound sterling and credited to OCBC's account with the Midland Bank in London.

While in Australia, Tan Chin Tuan had investigated ways to transfer the bank's records and assets there. Duplicates of all records had been prepared. One set was stored in OCBC's vaults, the other in an unobtrusive house near TCT's home, which also served as an air raid shelter and strongroom.

In early January, with the Japanese already in Johore, the directors of OCBC adopted a tactic initiated earlier by several corporations in Western Europe. If a company was no longer able to operate in its country of origin, it re-established its headquarters and registration in another country to thwart the German invaders. Availing itself of the Defence (Companies Temporary Transfer of Registered Office) Regulations, 1942, the directors of the OCBC had resolved to transfer the head office of the bank to Chungking, the war-time capital of Kuomintang China, where the OCBC had a branch. This would enable the bank to look after its branches in the unoccupied territories as well as its assets abroad. The overland route to Chungking was via Burma (Myanmar) where the bank had a branch in Rangoon (now Yangon).

The directors needed someone thoroughly trustworthy and competent to look after the bank's business during the uncertainty and chaos of war. They searched their ranks for their most senior men, but each of them, including OCBC's three general managers turned down this onerous task. Senior executives Kwa Siew Tee, Lim Bock Kee and Chew Hock Leong declined the assignment because they refused to leave their families behind. This made Tan Chin Tuan the inevitable choice.

Moreover, the strategies he devised and proposed to protect the bank's funds during the impending conflict were not lost on the directors. They also recognised that his high-profile public work on the Passive Defence Council and other government committees already put him at dire risk at the hands of the Japanese. Even his own mother urged him to leave Singapore. Furthermore, at the behest of the authorities, TCT had earlier safely evacuated his wife and three children to Australia. With the arguments so stacked against him, TCT was unable to decline the assignment.

Amid seas patrolled by Japanese submarines and skies filled with enemy aircraft, preparations were quickly made to establish TCT as the bank's external administrator-general.

On February 2, 1942, the directors of OCBC promoted Tan Chin Tuan to the position of managing director, holding the title jointly with the existing managing director, the more senior Tan Ean Kiam. At the age of thirty-three, he was also accorded commerce's most important symbol of trust — power of attorney — to conduct the bank's overseas affairs.

Grateful for Tan Chin Tuan's tireless service, the Financial Secretary, H. Weisburg, helped secure government priority air passage to Rangoon.

On February 4, in midnight darkness, Tan Chin Tuan left Singapore's Johnston Pier on a Sutherland flying boat bound for Batavia (now Jakarta), capital of the Dutch East Indies, where he would board the plane to Rangoon. He took comfort in the fact that Batavia's Allied Command base could serve as a point of contact if necessary.

Less than two weeks later, the unthinkable happened. Fortress Singapore surrendered. A mere nine weeks after the Japanese had begun their southward invasion of the Malaya peninsula, 80,000 British troops, most of whom had not fired a shot, had been defeated by a vastly outnumbered Japanese force. For those left behind in Singapore, the three-year reign of terror had begun.

TCT took temporary refuge in the home of his brother-in-law living in the Indonesian capital. But each day in Batavia seemed like a lifetime. The turmoil disrupted all flights and Tan Chin Tuan waited almost a month for a plane to Rangoon. Suddenly the city began emptying. He asked a British information officer why the people were leaving, but the official was not permitted to answer.

Concerned, he visited the British Consulate and spoke to the vice-consul general, who also was reluctant to respond. "I am a British subject," demanded TCT, "you must tell me." The official hesitated. "Well, if you must know, you'd be wise to go to the south of Java."

As the trains had stopped running, TCT attempted to hire a car. He searched all night in vain for a garage with a vehicle for rent. After a sparse meal of bread and cold tea, he slept fitfully.

Early the next morning he resumed his search, during which he met an Armenian diamond merchant also looking for transportation. In the spirit of co-operation, they exchanged addresses. Unable to find a vehicle, Tan Chin Tuan returned home. Later in the day he heard the approaching chugging of an old car. Out stepped the smiling diamond merchant, Harry Gregory. He had found a taxi, driven by an Indian, willing to take him. But the driver did not have enough petrol, as it was rationed. TCT's brother-in-law happened to have a few cans stored away for his own car. He shared the precious fuel with them, before leaving to join his family in Sukabumi. Tan Chin Tuan and Harry Gregory drove south.

Despite the gravity of the situation, TCT never lost his sense of humour. Suddenly, they were stopped at a checkpoint by soldiers brandishing their weapons, but after a while the travellers were waved on. As they resumed the journey, Gregory asked, "Were you not nervous, with all those guns pointing at us?"

"No," smiled TCT, "I was more afraid the soldiers might be nervous."

"Why would that bother you?" asked the diamond merchant. "Because," laughed the banker, "if they were nervous, they might press the machine guns' trigger by mistake."

Anxious to reach their destination, they drove through Bandung, once the Paris of the East, without stopping, then turned down to the south coast of Java, to a place called Tjilatjap. Here they discovered the dreadful news. All hope of proceeding to Rangoon had to be abandoned. Two days later, the British retreated from the Burmese capital. Rangoon's fall was followed by the Dutch surrender at their Indonesian capital on March 8, 1942. All the European-ruled mainland and islands of Southeast Asia were now under Japanese domination.

Tan Chin Tuan's only available choice was to secure passage on a dilapidated river steamer bound for Australia — a country still mostly untouched by the war. Travellers now had few options, and the anxious group who had boarded the boat were willing to risk several dangerous days at sea on a shabby, unseaworthy vessel for the relative safety of the Antipodes.

The *General Verspeck* had a shallow draft and was not designed for challenging the high seas. The ageing craft was also severely overloaded. Normally, it carried few passengers. But these were troubled times, and the captain was willing to squeeze extra paying customers aboard, including survivors from the warships the *Repulse* and the *Prince of Wales*, for a handful of cash.

Few ventured below deck, the most vulnerable of locations should the boat be attacked. The main deck overflowed with the weary and the wary. Most crowded together, a swarm of anxiety and fear. Yet no other ship could have protected its passengers so well. Although the Japanese soon detected the little boat and launched an attack, their torpedoes merely passed under the flat hull, swallowed by the ocean. Unscathed, the modest vessel steamed ahead. The weather also protected them. A heavy downpour prevented enemy aircraft from flying and discovering them. Finally, she encountered a Dutch navy corvette, which formed a welcome protective escort for the rest of the voyage.

On arrival in the West Australian port of Fremantle, grateful to be back on terra firma, TCT quickly travelled to Sydney for a warm reunion with his family. Unwilling to take advantage of leisure time justly earned, he quickly set up an OCBC office in George Street, in the same building as the Bank of New South Wales. Living and working in Australia, Tan Chin Tuan grew to respect its citizens. He felt a comradeship with this new land and its people. They had much in common, both being at the receiving end of British colonialism.

Fortunately, Australia had a leader with strength of purpose and the ability to unite the country during the dark World War II days. Prime Minister John Curtin dared to argue with Churchill. The British Prime Minister wished to divert Australian troops serving in the Middle East to Burma, but Curtin, correctly believing Burma to be lost, insisted on bringing his troops home to defend Australia's northern perimeters. Furthermore, he sought the co-operation of the United States and in early 1942, General Douglas MacArthur transferred his headquarters to Australia.

Like all great leaders, Curtin had a deep concern for his people and he suffered many sleepless nights when the convoy ships carrying Australian soldiers were returning through the Japanese submarine-infested waters of the Indian Ocean. Almost 100,000 Australians would die in battle. The worry and burden of war proved too much for Curtin, whose health steadily deteriorated. He died in office on July 5, 1945.

John Curtin's humanity was a trait shared by many Australian people, as Tan Chin Tuan and his family would discover during these years. Small gestures revealed large hearts. The stationmaster, knowing TCT's schedule, would hold the train a minute or two, should the banker be late. When he needed a new suit, but had no ration coupons, the local tailor, sympathetic to the problems of a refugee, willingly offered to make him a suit of fine English worsted, without the requisite stamps. TCT's young son, innocent of the national food conservation programme, asked for a dozen eggs at the grocery store. The grocer's wife, a Mrs Dorby, asked the boy to wait. Once the other customers left, she quietly explained that Australians were not allowed more than two to four eggs each. But with a smile she gave him a dozen anyway, saying, "Take it. You're a newcomer here and you don't keep hens. You deserve more eggs."

TCT reciprocated the Australians' kindness. He learned that all the rice produced in the country was reserved for the Asians taking refuge here. The Tan family was given a large ration of rice, far more than they needed. TCT made up half-pound packets of rice and presented them each month to a number of officials in the Bank of New South Wales, so the Australians could enjoy their favourite dessert — rice pudding.

Tan Chin Tuan quickly became the source of news from home for others from Singapore and Malaya, forced to spend the war in Australia. Many were in financial distress, as their bank accounts were frozen. TCT did what he could to help and to bolster their spirits, he often bought them dinner at Chinese restaurants.

Despite the relentless undercurrents of worry and concern for those at home, everyday life took on a welcome peacefulness. But after a year of this imposed tranquillity, Tan Chin Tuan grew increasingly anxious to complete his original plan for the bank.

When the Japanese invaded Burma, most of the officers of the OCBC branch in Rangoon escaped northwards with the branch's account books to Chungking, the wartime Chinese capital. Slumped on a mountain at the junction of two great rivers, Chungking was enduring continuous Japanese bombing raids.

An OCBC branch still functioned in this besieged but defiant city. With newspapers suggesting that the war had subsided somewhat in

Southeast Asia, Tan Chin Tuan decided it was as good a time as any to risk leaving the safety of Australia and resume his mission to establish the bank's international headquarters.

But with China cut off by sea and direct air routes, the only way to the inland capital was through India and over the Himalayan mountains. He immediately booked passage on a steamer leaving for Colombo, Ceylon (now Sri Lanka).

TCT left his wife and three children behind. The journey would be perilous and he would not jeopardise their safety. He secretly took out an insurance policy for 50,000 pounds sterling to provide for them should he die en route to India. The excessive five per cent premium confirmed the risk. To avoid alarming Helene, he entrusted the policy to the manager of the Bank of New South Wales, Harold Brown. With a heavy heart and moist eyes, Brown asked his fellow banker: "How can you go when it is so dangerous?" Tan Chin Tuan replied that duty took precedence over personal security.

Peck Pia Jim, the assistant manager of OCBC's Rangoon branch, had managed to escape with his family to Australia from Burma, so Tan Chin Tuan now had a travelling companion for the journey to Chungking. At the end of July 1943, the two men bid a heartfelt farewell to their families. They left by train for Fremantle, where they boarded a steamer, heading for South Asia and the Indian Ocean.

As the vessel set out to sea, Tan Chin Tuan stood quietly on the deck and watched the Australian coastline recede from the horizon. He knew there was no safe passage in these treacherous seas, with much of East and Southeast Asia under the military control of the Japanese. Like the untested boat, TCT was sailing into the unknown, embarking on a new and dangerous adventure.

Indian Sojourn

For about two weeks, the little boat bobbed precariously in the swirling sea. Huddled together, the passengers anxiously searched the violent waves for signs of enemy submarines — a silent predator, more deadly than the sharks cruising these dangerous waters.

Fearing attack, the crew ordered the passengers to wear their life jackets continuously and sleep on deck, never below. Strict blackout rules were observed, even to the extent of forbidding the lighting of cigarettes on deck at night. Travelling in a convoy of three steamers, the small vessels crept silently through the Indian Ocean. Tan Chin Tuan's boat was in the middle of the convoy.

An enemy submarine soon spotted the first steamer and torpedoes exploded into its hull. The Japanese commander was shocked by the unexpected and pitiful sight of women and children struggling in the water around the wreckage. Succumbing to compassion, he rescued the survivors and transferred them to land.

By the time the submarine returned, TCT's boat had slipped through to the safety of Ceylon. The remaining vessel wasn't as lucky. The Japanese commander, knowing there were women and children aboard, demanded its immediate surrender. The little boat and its passengers were captured without firing a shot.

Tan Chin Tuan arrived in Colombo in September 1943, relieved that the perilous journey was behind him and somewhat awestruck that his boat had miraculously avoided the fate of its two companion vessels. After a joyful reunion with his nieces, Yeo Kheng Sian and Yeo Oon Geok, TCT and his assistant, Peck Pia Jim, continued their journey to the Indian subcontinent and the Bengal city of Calcutta (now Kolkata).

This Indian city would provide several divergent but indelible lessons for the banker from Singapore. One was all too visible in its hot, dusty streets — the astonishing disparity between rich and poor. Bengal was experiencing one of its worst famines, due to the failure of the main rice crop harvested in the winter of 1942 and worsened by an absence of Burmese rice due to the war. The disaster would continue into 1944, killing 1.5 million people, a direct result of the famine itself and the epidemics that followed.

Calcutta's poverty shocked TCT, who was also horrified by the skeletal figures of the paupers, wobbling pathetically through the streets in search of food and money. At every intersection, the buses would be swarmed by beggars straining to reach into the windows. On every street, the poor would lean their exhausted wretched bodies against the walls, stretching their emaciated arms in a pitiable gesture for alms. The most desperate deliberately maimed their own children to provoke more sympathy.

From time to time, one member of this starving multitude would fall down dead on the road. Peck Pia Jim urged TCT to witness the cremation of a group of these corpses. An unforgettable image haunted those who watched the macabre spectacle. The roaring flames of the pyre dried the sinews in the limbs of the corpses, causing the burning cadavers to suddenly rise up inside the fire, as if they were still alive.

TCT had little respect for those wealthy Indians who callously drove in their limousines past people starving to death, en route to fashionable restaurants serving eighteen-course meals. It was in stark contrast to Australia with its spirit of generosity. Restaurant meals in the Antipodes were capped at four shillings and sixpence and food was carefully rationed so that everyone received his fair share. The Calcutta experience inspired compassion in Tan Chin Tuan toward those of little means and an acceptance of the responsibility of the strong and powerful to help the weak.

Within days of arriving in Calcutta, a message from an Inspector Lloyd summoned TCT and Peck Pia Jim to the Foreigners' Registration Office, to officially register themselves under the Registration of Foreigners Act of 1939. TCT was offended. The regulations unfairly confused Tan Chin Tuan's ethnicity with his nationality. He considered himself British and his support of the British colonial government in Singapore validated his loyalty to the crown. It was ridiculous that he should register as a foreigner.

Arriving at the Pretoria Street office, TCT met with an officious and unsympathetic immigration officer. His argument, that he was a British subject and deserved the protection, privileges and respect that his birthright assumed, was ignored. Instead, he was given a travel permit, requiring him to leave India within fifteen days. He was handed a copy of Ordinance XVI, 1942, which stated that the rules applied to "any person who was at birth a subject of any state in Europe excluding His Majesty's Dominions in Europe, or a Japanese, Chinese or Thai subject."

Tan Chin Tuan is not a man who would compromise his principles. He was not prepared to accept the improper and outrageous ordinance. Returning to the Royal Palace Hotel, he wrote to as many people of influence as he knew who might help champion his rights as a British subject. The principle went beyond one man's situation. He was offering himself as a precedent-setting case on behalf of all non-Caucasian British subjects.

The authorities continued to ignore his entreaties. Three days before the travel visa was to expire, TCT desperately sought legal assistance, engaging the services of Orr Dignam and Co. On September 28, the chief of the security police in Calcutta called a meeting. Tan Chin Tuan, accompanied by his lawyer, D.V. Irving-Jones, complied. At the police offices, a tyrannical Irishman named N. Tolson insisted that he register as an alien. TCT informed him that he was a British subject, that he carried a British passport and was therefore not subject to alien registration laws.

British citizenship held by a Chinese man meant nothing to Tolson. All he saw was an Oriental face, which meant only one thing — a foreigner. No amount of arguing by TCT or Jones could persuade the security policeman. Indeed, it only made him angrier. Finally he burst out: "All Chinese are shoemakers, restaurateurs and black marketeers!"

Without hesitation TCT shot back: "It would be equally true to say all Britishers are policemen." The remark infuriated Tolson, who shouted, "Get out!" to both men, leaving the matter unresolved. But it delighted TCT's legal counsel, who roared, patted him on the back and offered — from his point of view — the highest compliment, "Chin Tuan," Irving-Jones laughed, "you should be a lawyer."

The following day, TCT received a mysterious, yet compelling telegram, sent from Delhi. Its message was enigmatic: "Come.Important. Urgent." It was signed "John Galvin", a name which seemed vaguely familiar. Inquiring at the British Consulate in Calcutta, the first secretary, Stanley Smith, confirmed he had instructions to send Tan Chin Tuan immediately to the Indian capital. The diplomat had even booked rail passage for the banker and his assistant, Peck, underlining the importance of this mission. During wartime, all train travel was restricted.

As the train pulled into the Delhi railway station, Tan Chin Tuan spotted a man with a red moustache and red tie waiting on the platform. He looked familiar. Immediately TCT remembered him. John Galvin was a talented advertising agency artist from Singapore, who had designed advertisements for one of the bank's companies.

After the usual greetings, Galvin invited TCT and Peck to a Chinese restaurant. Over lunch, he leaned forward, stared into Tan Chin Tuan's eyes and whispered dramatically, "Do you want to die?"

TCT insisted that he did not. "The situation at the moment is that you are to be detained under the Defence of India Regulations," Galvin explained. TCT was stunned. The welcome meal was no longer palatable.

Later that day, Galvin escorted Tan Chin Tuan and Peck Pia Jim to the British Ministry of Information. By the demeanour of the sub-ordinates, TCT quickly realised that this man was much more powerful than a mere commercial artist. Galvin led them into a huge office, to a table presided over by a tall, angular Indian, the under-secretary of state for the Home Office. Galvin requested Tan Chin Tuan's classified file. "Here," Galvin said, handing the folder to TCT, "I want you to see this."

Reading his confidential file, TCT learned that the peevish and bigoted Tolson in Calcutta had recommended that the banker be detained as a subversive. Tan Chin Tuan reread the words several times, "to be detained as a subversive under the Defence of India Regulations". During wartime, under these regulations, no trial was necessary. His legs went limp. Indian prisons were notoriously lethal places. It was tantamount to a death sentence.

Unable to speak, a shaken TCT handed the secret folder back to Galvin, who assured him he need not worry. He wrote a few notes in TCT's file, personally vouching for both his integrity and loyalty to the British. This intervention might have saved Tan Chin Tuan's life.

Owing to his interest in Singapore, Galvin had been informed of TCT's case and had decided to intervene. But who was this clearly powerful man? Galvin led Tan Chin Tuan into the British Ministry of Information, where he was surprised to discover that Galvin was not only the deputy director of the British Ministry, but also Chief of the British Secret Service for the Far East.

Galvin was afraid that Tolson would find an excuse to detain the banker, so he gave TCT a letter appointing him an honorary adviser to the British Ministry of Information. Concerned that even this letter might not be enough protection, Galvin instructed TCT to telephone Stanley Smith daily. The diplomat was actually Galvin's undercover assistant. If and when TCT did not telephone Stanley Smith, the latter would call him. The daily phone calls continued until Tan Chin Tuan left Calcutta.

Although the danger had passed, TCT still had the original matter of his aliens' registration to resolve. It would have been easy for Tan Chin Tuan to register, as others had done. But his integrity and honour demanded action. He thought it was unjust that Caucasian British subjects were not required to register, but those of Oriental ancestry were. He continued the fight, maintaining that one who was born British could not have his birthright taken away. The Chinese consul general, who held the view that TCT had dual nationality, did not help matters.

Tan Chin Tuan had a clever riposte for this flawed point of view, "You claim because the Chinese consul general claims that I am a Chinese subject, that I am considered a Chinese subject in your eyes. Now, may I ask you, if the German radio was to broadcast a claim that Louis Mountbatten was a German, would you take away his command?"

TCT's strong feelings on this dispute were revealed in a thoughtful and prophetic letter written in October 1944 to his friend Tunku Abu Bakar, the second son of Sultan Ibrahim of Johore. As always, he saw the greater issue:

"It has been suggested that as the war may end before long, and that the inconvenience of such registration is only temporary, one should forbear. In my humble opinion, the question is not merely one of inconvenience; it is one of rights and principles. We are embroiled in this bloody and devastating war, not because of threat of immediate aggression, nor for gain. We did so on principle and to uphold the democratic conception of rights and freedom. To tolerate any violation of the birthright of citizenship is to acquiesce in undermining democracy. British Subjects of Chinese origin aggrieved by this discrimination must not be allowed to conclude that the Imperial Government is indifferent about their rights. In exile, few will dare to ventilate their grievance, but if they should return to their homes nursing such grievances, the repercussions will be widespread and irreparable."

Between September 1943 and August 1944, Tan Chin Tuan wrote more than seventy letters to Indian and British government officials. Finally, he achieved his goal. A letter written on August 5, from W.J.K. Stark, the Malayan Representative in India, officially delivered the news on behalf of C.D. Ahearne, the Special Representative of the Secretary of State for the Colonies. Responding to his perseverance and sound reasoning, the Government of India ruled that "British subjects of Chinese Origin, who possess British Passports issued in Malaya, are not subject to the provisions of the Foreigners Ordinance, 1942".

In the end, common sense prevailed and a principle was upheld. Tan Chin Tuan's name was finally removed from the alien registration lists. In addition, having fought on behalf of all Malaya-born British subjects, all his countrymen in India likewise benefited from his tenacity.

TCT was unaware the highest British authorities had noticed some of the letters he had written. They considered the banker from Singapore loyal to the British cause and trusted him completely. This was a departure from the prevailing attitude. Generally the British suspected the Chinese of playing a fickle double game, considering themselves British or Chinese if and when it suited them. But they had no such doubts about Tan Chin Tuan. In fact, they had a role for him to play. In December, 1943, the Colonial Secretary, S.W. Jones, who had been chairman when TCT served on the Passive Defence Committee, sent a letter from Bournemouth, England, to Edward Gent, head of the Eastern Department in Britain's Colonial Office. It illustrates the kind of decisions that the British often made behind the scenes.

"Dear Gent,

"I have just received a letter from a Singapore Chinese, Tan Chin Tuan, in which he offers his services to the cause of rehabilitating Malaya under British control. He writes c/o the Chartered Bank, Calcutta, and he himself held a very important position in the Oversea-Chinese Bank in Singapore. He says that Weisberg helped him to get away from Singapore on February 4th, 1942, in order that he might take charge of the HQ of his bank, which had been transferred to India. This is what he says:

"I feel that as I am practically the only one amongst the Chinese Unofficial Representatives on the Governmental Organisations in Malaya, who is luckily out of the enemies' hands, it may be my duty to place my services at the disposal of the British Government... I am not a Military man, but my experience and knowledge of Malaya, particularly Singapore, may be of some use. I do not expect any remuneration since, as Managing Director of the Bank, I am more or less solely responsible for safeguarding the assets and re-establishing the institution in Malaya and elsewhere, and I can only undertake work which will still enable me to look after the Bank.

"On the other hand, it will be advantageous to let me retain my connection with the Bank because it had branches all over Malaya and was therefore more closely in touch with the population than any other organisation. My knowledge as Managing Director of Eastern Realty Co, which owned rubber estates and houses and landed properties all over the peninsula, may also prove of value.

Jones continued:

"I strongly recommend that Tan Chin Tuan be given a part in the organisation for the restoration of Malaya. He is one of the younger leading Chinese of Singapore and did a lot of most valuable work in connection with the preparations for the Civil Defence of Singapore. He had a large part in recruiting hundreds of Chinese for civil defence and, as one of the Chinese representatives on the Singapore Committee, which functioned most admirably in directing Civil Defence activities, I found him very helpful, very genuine and very frank and independent in his views. I came to hold him in high esteem and I should like to think that some day he will be chosen to play a prominent part in the political affairs of the Colony. I have a poor opinion of most of the senior Chinese public men in the Colony and I would certainly not go out of my way to recommend them for any part in Malaya's future. But Tan Chin Tuan is different and I think it would be wise to give him every possible encouragement.

"There is another point. In the earlier evacuations, the Chinese Banks were treated very badly. The British Banks were given warning and assistance; the Chinese Banks were overlooked. In consequence, they suffered heavy losses. A suitable gesture of friendship and encouragement to this representative of the most important of the Chinese Banks might serve to assuage some of the hard feelings which they undoubtedly felt..."

This recommendation by the British to find a prominent role for TCT would prove important in the transition years as British rule receded. But more consequential was the fact that the British considered him completely trustworthy. He could speak out with impunity. Unlike other Chinese, he could now criticise without his loyalty being questioned.

During his sojourn in Calcutta, TCT learned that Chang Kia Ngau, the former general manager of the Bank of China, would be visiting the city. TCT greatly respected Chang, never forgetting the time when he graciously withdrew, allowing the completion of the OCBC merger in 1932.

Chang had become increasingly unhappy with the Chiang Kai-shek government. Foreseeing the final victory of the communists, he left China to go to the United States, stopping in Calcutta en route.

Chang sent a message through the Chinese consul general that he would like to see TCT. When Tan Chin Tuan entered the room, he noticed it was full of generals and dignitaries seeking to meet Chang. TCT sat quietly in a corner. Within minutes, Chang's secretary approached him, saying, "Mr Chang will see you now." Chang, in fact, met up with him for almost one week. Tan Chin Tuan was invited to lunch and dinner, and accompanied Chang to several large functions as his guest. The two men became staunch friends.

Chang finally managed to travel to the United States from India. While there, he studied ways China could accelerate post-war economic development. In late 1945, he was asked by the Chiang Kai-shek government to return to China. The KMT government appointed him chairman of the North-East (Manchuria) Economic Commission, until March 1947, when he was appointed governor of the Central Bank of China. However, when the communist forces overran China, Chang decided to leave. He spent three years in Australia, before returning to the United States. There, he taught at Loyola University until joining

Stanford University's prestigious Hoover Institution on War, Revolution and Peace.

In December 1943, Tan Chin Tuan left Calcutta for the western coastal city of Bombay. Here, he learned that bankers in Chungking were under immense pressure from the Chinese Nationalist government to provide funding. The government threatened to shoot those who refused to comply. As it was critical to establish the bank outside Singapore to thwart any Japanese control, he thought it would be foolish to exchange one perilous situation for another.

TCT decided to re-establish the OCBC in Bombay instead. Initially, India's laws prevented re-registration, but after some legal amendments, the bank was officially re-registered in January 1945. Joined by his assistant, Peck Pia Jim, Tan Chin Tuan set up offices in Bombay's Central Bank Building in Esplanade Road. They printed cheques and assembled refugee bank officers from Rangoon, Shanghai and Hong Kong. With the bank able to function, TCT then called a general meeting of refugee shareholders. The Oversea-Chinese Banking Corporation was back in business.

Now settled in Bombay, TCT became active in two groups. He was appointed vice-president of the Oversea-Chinese Association (Bombay). The OCBC director and Straits Settlements Executive Council member, Tan Cheng Lock had founded the Bombay OCA. Tan Chin Tuan also joined the Malayan Association, which served both as a social club for expatriates and a benevolent organisation for refugees. Lawyer John Laycock, Singapore Municipal Commissioner Joe Elias, Tunku Abu Bakar and H. Fancott had founded the association. But the four men had quarrelled and divided into factions. TCT pleaded, "We are already without a country. Let us not fight, let's try and work together."

His peacemaking inevitably led to his being elected chairman. In this capacity, he helped distressed refugees from Singapore and Malaya. In one instance, TCT asked a Malayan government representative in India to approach the British government regarding the plight of two young medical students. Miss Oon Chiew Seng and Miss Loh Siew Geck were stranded in India after Malaya fell to the Japanese. With TCT's intervention, the two women eventually reached Britain, where they completed their studies.

The Malayan Association kept its expatriate community informed and encouraged by way of a regular newsletter, which reported happenings from the occupied territories. Monthly get-togethers were organised at local hotels. The orchestras, singers and familiar tunes raised people's spirits and were a welcome respite from the pressure of war and the tedium of impoverished India.

Tan Chin Tuan would soon have more than the camaraderie of fellow refugees. He was reunited with his wife, Helene, and their children in 1944. John Galvin had not only arranged for their safe passage from Australia, but also vouched for their bona fides. The family rented a large apartment in Cumbala Hill, a fashionable Bombay neighbourhood. Here, TCT spent happy hours, bouncing his youngest daughter on his knee while she sang her favourite songs.

Finally, the glorious news arrived. The war was over. On August 14, 1945, United States President Harry Truman and Japanese Emperor Hirohito announced on a simultaneous broadcast that Japan had surrendered. General Douglas MacArthur, Supreme Commander of the Allied Powers, had accepted the surrender of the Japanese forces. The formal document was signed in Tokyo on September 2.

In Singapore, a few dejected generals, their uniforms tattered, their troops in shambles, were ordered by Emperor Hirohito's envoy to suspend all military activity. On September 12, the Supreme Allied Commander for Southeast Asia, Admiral Lord Louis Mountbatten, accepted the surrender of the Japanese forces in Singapore.

In India, the newspapers were filled with the joyous news. Wiping away a tear, TCT read of Singapore's jubilant, three-mile victory parade from Empire Dock to the Cathay Building. Apparently, the participants could not wait for the formal documentation and celebrated the peace a week before Mountbatten received the official surrender. TCT longed to be home and he did not have to wait long.

With the cessation of hostilities, control of the occupied territories of the Far East returned to their respective governments. TCT and three other bankers, Mr J.H. Kortwright from the Chartered Bank of India, Australia and China; Mr R.A. Stuart of the Hongkong and Shanghai Bank; and the Mercantile Bank's Mr Stanley Stocks, were told to leave for Singapore without delay. Under the auspices of the Civil Affairs section of the British Military Administration, they were to re-establish banking facilities, vital to the revival of the island's economy.

Getting home proved both difficult and time-consuming. The Indian officials instructed the bankers to proceed to Madras in southern India, where they waited for a week. Next, they were told to move on to Colombo. TCT took a station wagon across the Palk Strait to the beautiful and verdant island, which even in wartime was a tree-covered paradise. Here, Tan Chin Tuan waited again with his colleagues from the other banks. Suddenly, military officials ordered them to go immediately to the northeastern port of Trincomalee.

Upon arrival, tired and hungry, they reported to the officer-in-charge of the British RAF station who demanded to know why they were late. Their explanations of sluggish Indian bureaucracy fell on deaf ears. They attempted to snatch an overdue meal in the air force canteen, but it was interrupted by the same officer, who told them impatiently, "You have got to go now because I've got A1 priority given to you." They also learned that several passengers had been forced to give up their seats for them. This sudden importance surprised the bankers, coupled with relief that they were finally going home.

At midnight, on September 14, 1945, the four bankers boarded a Dakota flying boat. The uncomfortable plane made its take off run across the Trincomalee harbour, but failed to achieve lift off. TCT asked one of the crew what was wrong and learned that the plane was severely overloaded. But by the time the crew tried a second run, the plane burned sufficient fuel to lighten the plane, allowing it to become airborne.

The following day, a month after the Japanese surrender and nine days after the British had resumed control of Singapore and Malaya, the plane carrying Kortwright, Stuart, Stocks and Tan touched down at Seletar Airbase. It was an emotional homecoming. Giddy with relief, tears eclipsed the laughter. The only glum faces were the Japanese prisoners who carried the bankers' suitcases.

Although the returning bankers thought they had mentally prepared themselves, the sight of a Singapore devastated by forty-three months of war and occupation still shocked them. The streets were lined with buildings bearing signs completely in Japanese — the compulsory language of the occupation. The Japanese Kempeitai, or secret police, had terrorised and tortured civilians. Food was scarce and diseases rampant, despite frequent Japanese sanitation campaigns.

But now the war was over, it was time for renewal and rebuilding. Downtown, a faded Union Jack, long hidden in the infamous Changi Prison, flew over City Hall. Finally, hope replaced despair. For Singapore and its people, it was a new beginning.

Restoration

For three and a half years, the population of Singapore had endured Japanese domination. Contrary to the stated intention by the government in Tokyo to be conciliatory, her conquerors were ruthless. The Japanese army used atrocities such as torture, rape and the grisly sight of decapitated heads impaled on posts, to terrorise the population into submission.

During the occupation, Europeans, considered Japan's principal enemy, were automatically put in internment camps. Of the remaining ethnic groups, the Chinese were singled out for the most brutality. This maltreatment was rationalised as retribution for several alleged transgressions — ferocity of the brave Dalforce fighters, support of China's cause and unspoken anti-Japanese hostility. The 25th Army was particularly savage. Unprovoked kicks and slaps to defenceless Chinese residents were commonplace and in sharp contrast to a perceived benevolence toward Malays and Indians.

Japanese failure to maintain commerce throughout the occupation years had virtually ruined Singapore. But economic hardships in uncertain times inspire resourceful solutions. Rationing and food shortages encouraged people to grow their own tapioca, yams, sweet potatoes and vegetables. Those who could not generate a meagre living sold cherished possessions to provide the money to survive. A few collaborated with the enemy.

Hyperinflation in the final months of the Occupation had ravaged the economy. The son of OCBC's vice-chairman Lee Choon Seng had paid $1,500 for a single fish and $30 for two large bananas. People were out of work and penniless. The malnutrition resulting from such poverty led to epidemics such as beri beri and malaria. The sanitation infrastructure was in tatters — improvements to sewage disposal and water purification were urgently needed.

After the war, the statutory responsibilities for the reconstruction and revival of Singapore fell on the British Military Administration (BMA), which governed Malaya for seven months, until colonial rule was re-established by the appointment of a new governor-general. But having suffered due to Britain's inability to protect them, the population lost faith in the system. A spirit of self-reliance was awakening.

To the returning Tan Chin Tuan, Singapore looked nothing like the orderly and beautiful city he had left. Bicycles, carts and a few army vehicles rattled through the broken streets. He missed the sounds of the bustling traffic. The roads were almost devoid of private cars and trucks. With few parts available in wartime, the rusted hulks of abandoned trucks testified to the decay. The country had been violated. Familiar places appeared distorted by the carnage of war — damaged buildings, shattered structures and crumbling debris.

The home he returned to was empty. During the Occupation, TCT's beautiful white house on Cairnhill Road had been taken over by a Japanese commander. Shortly before the invaders surrendered to the British, the officer had given the entire contents of the home, including the furniture, to his servants. Abandoned and neglected, only two items survived, a small table and a straight-backed teak chair, which TCT keeps, as a reminder, to this day. Tan Chin Tuan had no choice but to accept the generosity of OCBC's general manager, Chew Hock Leong, for his nightly refuge.

Within two weeks of his return to Singapore, TCT was asked to Government House for a luncheon with Lord Louis Mountbatten, the Supreme Commander for the Allied Forces in Southeast Asia. The invitation provided a rare moment of mirth in these sombre times. Even Government House had suffered Japanese plundering and none of its elegant dinnerware had survived the occupation. The staff desperately borrowed dishes and utensils from local hotels for this important occasion. The guests were served their food on crockery and silverware bearing the logos of The Raffles and The Adelphi. Lord Mountbatten asked Tan Chin Tuan if he was enjoying the meal. TCT politely replied, "Yes," paused, then added mischievously, "and on stolen property!" The guests roared with laughter. Mountbatten, charmed by the response, from that day forth referred to TCT as "that cheeky fellow".

Government House's devastation represented the state of Singapore in 1945. The colony urgently required a few good men to contribute their talents to revive prosperity and optimism. Amid formidable challenges and new political awakenings, the shattered community needed wise and competent leaders. One of the men they would increasingly turn to in the months ahead was Tan Chin Tuan.

TCT's first responsibility, however, was to the bank. The situation was critical. OCBC had lost $2.5 million between the British surrender in 1942 and the Japanese surrender in 1945. The bank also lost more than a tenth of its 280 staff members, killed during the occupation. Tan Ean Kiam, who was joint managing director, passed away in 1943. Overseas branches had been closed.

TCT requested a meeting with Lee Choon Seng, the bank's vice-chairman. He wanted to offer his resignation as joint managing director, believing there were more senior men in the bank who rightly were in line for the position. But, with good reason, none of them wished to tackle the monumental challenge of rebuilding OCBC. Lee Choon Seng and the chairman, Lee Kong Chian, insisted TCT accept the responsibility. Thus, at the age of thirty-seven, Tan Chin Tuan began the task of rehabilitating and revitalising OCBC.

As sole managing director, Tan Chin Tuan was instructed, along with the European bankers, to report immediately to the financial secretary. Due to his nominal rank of captain, TCT wore the military uniform that was *de rigueur* for those working in an official capacity under the British Military Administration. At this crucial meeting, the financial secretary revealed Singapore's fiscal plight — not only were all the banks in crisis, but the colony's entire financial affairs were also in shambles.

During the occupation, the Japanese had kept the banks open by decree, forcing the officers and local staff to co-operate with them, often under duress. Customers with credit balances drew on them. People who had debit balances either paid them down, or drew out more money. It was a time of complete banking chaos. In addition, the banks were forced to deal in Japanese Occupation government-issued currency, denominated between one cent and $1,000, but without any backing in actual assets.

When the British resumed control of Singapore on September 5, 1945, they declared the Japanese currency (which carried no serial numbers) invalid. To prevent panic, they closed all the banks during the confusing transfer of authority from September 5 to September 17. Their proclamation fundamentally rendered all the banks, including OCBC, insolvent. Both of OCBC's immense vaults overflowed with these worthless "banana notes", so named because the ten dollar note depicted a banana plant.

The BMA quickly prepared the new bank-notes which had been printed in Britain for distribution. But the currency required a carefully synchronised distribution to avoid a monetary crisis. The authorities told TCT that it was of the utmost importance to reopen OCBC at the same time as the British banks in Singapore. This was to avoid what one military official tactfully described as "unnecessary difficulty in re-establishing internal trade and tranquillity".

The request was also an unspoken acknowledgment of how important the bank, and the Chinese business community it served, had become. OCBC had the distinction of being the first local bank to receive the new British currency, due to TCT's close and cordial relationship with the British. It was now managing director Tan Chin Tuan's responsibility to make certain that the Oversea-Chinese Banking Corporation was ready to open.

Everything OCBC had built up in the years between the 1932 merger that formed it and the outbreak of war, had disappeared. The senior staff were divided by misunderstandings and bitterness. Bitterness towards those who took refuge abroad from those who had suffered the occupation. Bitterness towards those who co-operated, albeit through fear and intimidation, from those who suffered unduly from Japanese atrocities. Bitterness against those whom fate spared from those who lost family and property.

As an impartial onlooker, Tan Chin Tuan acted as both peacemaker and counsellor. His reputation for fairness and integrity encouraged the staff and officers to work harmoniously together and drew old and new customers to the bank.

The one person, it could be argued, who was not fairly treated was the managing director himself, who only drew a $600 per month salary. TCT argued that as the bank was almost bankrupt, and since he had his own personal wealth, he did not need the usual, generous compensation afforded bank executives. Later, as the bank prospered, its chairman, Lee Kong Chian, proposed an increased salary plus a percentage of profit. However, TCT limited his own salary to a maximum of $600,000 per year and bonuses equivalent to less than half Lee Kong Chian's original recommendation.

Tan Chin Tuan's management style immediately made its mark by forbidding nepotism. The bank needed to quickly hire and train staff to fill the many vacant positions. Traditionally, directors would send their sons to the bank for jobs. TCT put a stop to this. As he later recalled in an interview with the magazine, Euromoney:

> "When I was quite junior, I was aware that some of the staff were dissatisfied because they feared that a director's or a senior officer's son was likely to be treated preferentially. This was not the fault of the former management. It was simply the perpetuation of an old Chinese tradition. But this made the more promising bank officers feel that they might do better to seek other pastures. To set a good example, I therefore did not allow my son or my brother to join the bank. It was a painful decision."
>
> — The Tide in the Life of Tan Chin Tuan, October 1982

This act of leadership extinguished any grumbling from the other directors and thereafter, all new employees were carefully screened and hired on the basis of competence, not connections.

Next, he implemented new rules to ensure the bank's survival. One related to the issue of loan recommendations. Previously, Chinese banks had often been used as "old boys' clubs", where loans were automatically extended to friends of the officers or directors. Now, if directors wished to recommend their friends for large loans, they had to guarantee repayment personally. There were no exceptions — even the chairman had to comply. When Lee Kong Chian promised a loan to a Malayan politician, he was asked to co-sign it according to TCT's instructions. Ousted from power, the politician defaulted, obliging the OCBC chairman to repay the debt himself.

TCT also introduced a code of ethics to assure the bank's debtors that should they default and their security sold, the directors and officers of the bank would abstain from purchasing the assets. In addition, he discouraged taking a stake in a customer's company, ensuring that the bank would not be influenced by that investment to act against the bank's best interests.

The end of the war produced both happy reunions and sorrowful memories. Few escaped persecution or deprivation. Many of TCT's European friends and government colleagues suffered at the brutal hands of the Japanese. Between 80 and 90 per cent of the Malayan Civil Service had been imprisoned. One of TCT's most haunting memories was the sight of a skeletal man, sleeping in a Bengali-style charpoy bed, wearing nothing but rags. Emaciated and broken, he bore little resemblance to the once magisterial Lazarus Rayman, who had served as municipal president in the late 1930s. TCT's mentor and friend Rayman had spent the war in barbaric conditions in a Singapore prisoner-of-war camp.

Tan Chin Tuan has always been a man of action. He showed his deep compassion for those who had suffered in practical ways. He recognised people's need for financial help. He instituted a process to ensure that penniless former internees, many of whom were roaming the streets in tatters, could receive interest-free loans of $500 to $1,000. (The offer was made to civilians only, as servicemen were looked after by the military.) He required no collateral, merely a promise to repay when they had the means to do so. In total, the bank lent $100,000 to former civilian prisoners. Remarkably, only two loans were not repaid, both due to the death of the borrowers.

At first glance, this magnanimity might have appeared to be a leap of faith, because the British Military Administration had stipulated that all money advanced to the banks, had to be repaid in full at a later date. However, the bank's generosity would pay off in more tangible terms. TCT's loan policy not only generated goodwill, but also attracted new, loyal customers. By granting loans to old and new businesses and putting currency into circulation, it also helped stimulate the dormant Singapore economy.

As noted earlier, the war had touched everyone, even the wealthy. One of Singapore's most colourful businessmen was the memorable Aw Boon Haw. The Tiger Balm king had made a pre-war fortune with his popular all-purpose ointment. Aw was also a powerful shareholder in OCBC. Shortly after the war, TCT noticed that Aw had started selling his shares. Paying Aw a visit, he asked deferentially, "Uncle," (the two men were not related, this was a respectful honorific) "may I ask why you are selling your shares in the bank? Have you no confidence in us?" Aw replied that he needed start-up money to reopen his Tiger Balm factories, which had shut down during the war. Tan Chin Tuan suggested he take an overdraft instead. "I don't want to borrow money," insisted Aw. "It's not borrowing," said TCT. "I don't want to give security," Aw protested. No security was needed, TCT assured him. The banker tried to ascertain how much money Aw Boon Haw required, but the Tiger Balm king was reluctant to divulge this information. Exceeding his lending authority four-fold, TCT offered Aw a $2 million overdraft facility.

TCT reported this meeting to OCBC's chairman. He was convinced that Tiger Balm would enjoy the same success it had pre-war. Lee Kong Chian supported TCT's bold move. Aw did not sell his bank shares, overdrew only $500,000 and repaid it within a year. But his loyalty to OCBC lasted a lifetime. Decades later, Lee Chee Shan, the son-in-law of Aw's brother, started the Chung Khiaw Bank in Singapore. He urged Aw Boon Haw to transfer his funds to the new institution. Aw replied, "My money will never leave OCBC."

The bank also assisted its less powerful customers. It encouraged small savings accounts among wage earners in Singapore — clerks, maidservants, salesmen and even rickshaw pullers. These Chinese-speaking people stayed away from European banks, which demanded business be done in a foreign tongue. As TCT wrote in 1945, they wanted something more "familiar and less Olympian". He argued that the British Military Administration should ease the bank's reopening, since its repayment of deposits (even those made during the Japanese occupation) would do far more for these ordinary people than distributing free food, clothing and other forms of charity.

The kindness that Tan Chin Tuan showed to those in need inspired loyalty and gratitude. One former Australian prisoner of war received money to return home. There, he secured an agency for the Life Guard milk brand, a product he exported to the hungry market in Singapore. Years later, a European couple visited Singapore and asked to see TCT. The strangers told him that the Australian agent had died and that they had inherited, and wished to maintain, his milk exporting business. However, the Australian had willed them his business only on the condition that they promised to continue to bank with OCBC!

Once the bank was running smoothly in Singapore, TCT turned his attention to its extensive branch network in other territories. Reopening the foreign branches had a symbiotic effect for both the bank and the local communities. Even before the war had ended, TCT had noted in a lengthy memo to the British authorities that the predominantly ethnic Chinese rice millers of Burma were long-standing customers of OCBC's Rangoon branch. Since Burma, along with Siam (now Thailand) and Indo-China were major rice-exporting countries, it was imperative to get the millers back on their feet to alleviate region-wide food shortages. The millers, for their part, turned to OCBC, because it spoke and wrote Chinese to them at a time when European banks were interested only in European commerce.

Tan Chin Tuan also played an equally important role in Malaya's revival and development, both as a banker and a legislator. There were few European banks outside the major towns. The OCBC had six branches in a 350-kilometre area south of Seremban. This territory consisted of mostly rural and small to medium-size traders. OCBC was critical to their refinancing and recovery. Later, the colonial government of the Federation of Malaya, strapped for funds, turned to the government of Singapore for a loan of $30 million. At the third session of the Second Legislative Council on November 24, 1953, TCT proposed the loan and suggested it be granted interest-free for the first ten years.

His motion included these words, which succinctly demonstrates his philosophy and acute sense of balance and fairness:

> "During the last week or two, there has been much speculation in the Press on what Singapore should or would do to help the Federation. As a banker, I naturally deprecate such speculations. As always happens, those who have indulged in this unnecessary speculation have jumped to wrong conclusions; and others who have been too eager to air their views have merely initiated a useless controversy.

> "Many are inclined to be ultra generous in giving out of the pockets of others; but as the representatives of the people it is the duty of the Councillors to remember that the public funds of the Colony are not theirs to dispose of as they like. They must carefully balance the justification of voting away a large part of the Colony's surplus assets against the need of giving a helping hand to a good neighbour.

> "A gift of $5 million, as suggested in the Press, would make little, if any, difference to our good neighbour's finances; and bearing in mind that we are dealing with public funds and not our own, it would be improper to vote a bigger gift without the special approval of the taxpayer. It is, therefore, after careful consideration that I have come to submit this proposal before you.

> "$30 million may not appear to be much beside the $500 million which is the approximate annual estimated expenditure of the Federation for next year; but it is quite a lot to Singapore. It represents about 14 per cent of our total annual revenue, or nearly the whole of our estimated receipts from Tobacco Duties, the second largest item in our estimates of revenue. Moreover, as this loan is to be interest free for ten years, it represents, in effect, a gift of $14.25 million in interest if calculated at the current rate of 4.75 per cent.

> "However, the Colony can afford to make this gesture of friendship to the Federation. As Your Excellency has stated, the making of this loan will not retard our educational programme and the expansion of our social welfare services. In making this loan we may be giving away something which some of our City Councillors covet; but on the other hand, there is no merit in giving what is not wanted.

> "Sir, as the senior unofficial member and with the concurrence of my unofficial colleagues, I do now formally move the motion standing in my name."

Amid applause, the motion was adopted and the loan approved.

This thoughtfulness and fairness are the hallmarks of Tan Chin

Tuan's business philosophy. He insisted that the bank treat all customers honourably. One branch in Malaya sent in a proposal for a $30,000 loan from a man, who had a house worth $50,000, which he had offered as security. TCT was upset to learn that the branch was proposing to charge an excessive 18 per cent per annum on the loan, when it already had the home as collateral. "He's happy to pay it" was the response from the branch manager, eager to make as much interest for OCBC as possible. "But I'm not happy to receive it," TCT replied. "Reduce the rate to 12 per cent." Reluctantly, the branch manager obeyed. He telephoned the customer and said somewhat ambiguously, "My managing director wouldn't approve it." The borrower misinterpreted the branch manager's comment and thought he had been rejected. He grew angry. "He wouldn't approve the loan?" he asked in disbelief. "No," said the manager, "he wouldn't approve the interest rate. He said it was too high."

Years later, Tan Chin Tuan was waiting in a reception room at the Malaysian Ministry of Finance. A man approached him and introduced himself as that very customer whose loan rate TCT had reduced. He stated he had wanted to meet the banker in person to express his admiration for TCT's principles. He had never forgotten this incident and ever since had enthusiastically recommended OCBC to his friends and colleagues. He mentioned one other fact — he was Malaysia's Attorney-General.

Another issue requiring immediate action after the war involved the closing of branches in the former Dutch East Indies. Local activists unilaterally declared the archipelago independent from the Netherlands, forming the country of Indonesia. Ethnic tensions erupted quickly afterwards and the Indonesian authorities were eager to close foreign banks.

With the approval of the board of directors, TCT closed branches in Palembang, Djambi, Surabaya and later, Batavia. The Indonesian rupiah was falling in value and the government forbade OCBC to retain whatever profits it was making. Because funds transfers were restricted, TCT converted much of the bank's assets into gems, jewellery and precious stones. Instead of money, the staff was paid with office equipment, mainly typewriters. With the rupiah depreciating, office equipment became extremely valuable for resale and the employees benefited.

At the same time that TCT was re-establishing OCBC's reputation, he would also play a role in the reformation of Singapore itself. The devastation caused by war was not only physical. There was a sense of deep sorrow in the populace and an urgent need for stability and wise leadership.

The British turned to Tan Chin Tuan. His relationship with Lord Mountbatten had served to raise his prestige further. He was appointed to the Advisory Council of the British Military Administration. His access to the important figures in the BMA, such as the Chief Civil Affairs Officer, Sir Ralph Hone, and the civilian government that followed in 1946, would help gain concessions for his people.

TCT also had the support of prominent members of the Chinese community, whose co-operation was essential for the restoration of normalcy. Tan Kah Kee, for example, who had returned to Singapore at the end of the war, was a hero to the overseas Chinese for his work in raising money to aid China in its war against Japan. TCT relied on Tan Kah Kee's tremendous moral authority to ensure that food was fairly distributed. The British authorities appealed to the Chinese Advisory Board to recommend to their community to refrain from dining on suckling pig, a popular banquet fare, so that the piglets could mature to feed even more people. But many affluent Chinese wished to celebrate liberation with suckling pig banquets.

As Tan Kah Kee spoke no English, the British asked TCT to be their intermediary and enlist the hero's support in a campaign to temporarily stop the practice. Tan Kah Kee agreed. One evening, at the Ee Ho Hean Club, where Tan Kah Kee lived, he and TCT were invited to a dinner of a hundred guests. At Tan Kah Kee's insistence, TCT sat at his table. When the banquet hosts served suckling pig, Tan Kah Kee not only refused to eat it, he stood up angrily and stomped out. The press reported his reaction and suckling pig was quickly removed from the menus. The British authorities not only appreciated Tan Kah Kee's efforts, but also TCT's ability to influence and involve the important members of his community.

Tan Chin Tuan was also called upon to help solve another sensitive issue concerning the Chinese — the problem of Dalforce. During the Japanese invasion of Singapore, the commando units of the former Johore chief of police served with distinction. Positioned in the north-western section of the island, John D. Dalley's fighters used guerrilla tactics to disrupt the Japanese onslaught and slow its advance. But defeat was inevitable. Some of them were captured; others disappeared into the jungle for the duration of the war, to form the Malayan People's Anti-Japanese Army (MPAJA).

Nervous about communist dissenters threatening colonialism, the British ordered the MPAJA soldiers to come in from the Malayan jungle and lay down their weapons. The soldiers demanded payment for their wartime participation. But the authorities could not agree on what the former members of Dalforce should be paid for their service to the Crown. In addition, there were others from Singapore and Malaya who had also fought bravely, but the haste of war provided no official proof of the amount of time they served fighting for the cause. Both sides' positions became entrenched and the exasperated British turned to TCT to mediate.

Tan Chin Tuan was prepared to help the government deal with the Dalforce soldiers. But the colonial government insisted there could be no negotiation while the MPAJA fighters remained armed. Eventually, those who gave up their arms were paid. The others just disappeared into the jungle, forming a guerrilla band that was to harass the British for more than a decade.

One of the most disturbing issues TCT had to face immediately after the war was the accusation that some of the leading Chinese in Singapore had been collaborators. Among them was Dr Lim Boon Keng, the former chairman of the Oversea-Chinese Bank and an early director of OCB. He had also served on the Legislative Council of the Straits Settlements between 1895 and 1905. The distinguished Dr Lim had been designated leader of the Chinese in Singapore by the Japanese. He was forced to serve as Chairman of the Overseas Chinese Association (Syonan) Fund-Raising Project and ordered to raise a total of $50 million throughout Malaya, as a mandatory gift to Japan for the war effort. Singapore's portion of the contribution was set at $10 million. Lim suffered severe duress, caught between his loyalty to the bank, the British and the unrelenting demands of the Japanese.

The British ordered the detention of all Chinese who had co-operated with the Japanese, including Lim. Tan Chin Tuan owed his life to Dr Lim, a former Queen's Scholar, whose medical skills had snatched TCT from certain death when he was a young child and seriously ill. TCT knew this kind, gentle man would never have betrayed Singapore. TCT also learned that several Chinese bankers in occupied Singapore had been similarly intimidated. The brutal Japanese troops had conducted a methodical programme of cruelty, torture and arbitrary executions. The Japanese demands for funds so distressed Lim Boon Keng that to escape the ordeal he would often pretend to be drunk.

Mindful of the impossible situation his colleagues had faced, TCT went directly to the Chief Civil Affairs Officer, Sir Ralph Hone. "Had you been here, under the threat of death, what would you have done?" he inquired. He also reminded Sir Ralph of the atrocities at the hands of the Japanese. "They rounded up Singapore residents from the concentration camps, sent able-bodied men to dig trenches as mass graves, then fired their machine guns and slaughtered them. Soldiers seized women and raped them. There was no law." Furthermore, TCT pointedly added, the bankers were forced to obey the Japanese in the wake of Britain's utter inability to defend the local populace.

The issue of Japanese brutality was close to TCT's heart. He had lost two nephews, two maternal uncles and many good friends during the Occupation. The injustice angered him. Citizens who had struggled to survive under the Japanese in the absence of their British protectors were now to be persecuted by the very people who had failed them.

Tan Chin Tuan suggested that the British authorities only arrest and punish those who had intentionally tried to harm others. Victor Purcell, the adviser on Chinese affairs, and the governor supported his position. With such powerful allies, TCT persuaded the British to stop the prosecution of many Chinese residents, including Dr Lim.

The reckless attempt to arrest innocent Chinese accelerated the feeling of disillusionment toward the British after the war. When civilian rule was restored in 1946, the British attempted to resume their cavalier imperial ways. But something had changed in the local population's hearts and minds.

The British no longer seemed infallible and omnipotent. The military catastrophe of 1942 revealed their feet of clay. They had been defeated by an Asian army with cunning, skill and, even worse, bluff. Malaya, including Singapore, was not eager to replace Japanese governance with a return to British colonialism. The memories of enslaved European masters, performing forced labour, could never be erased. The image of the cowed British, emaciated and in rags, shattered their aura of invincibility. Tan Chin Tuan sensed that things would never be the same. Singapore and Malaya now had the will and the self-confidence to seek independence. The soft sea breezes that blew across the green field of Singapore's Padang carried the seeds of change.

Public Service, Political Upheaval

The dangers facing Singapore in the decade following World War II were in many ways more perilous than the three and a half years of brutal Japanese occupation. The events that transpired in those critical early post-war years would have far more lasting effects. Events propelled Tan Chin Tuan into public life at a time when the right men were needed to guide the course of history.

New political parties appeared. The Malayan Democratic Union (MDU) was founded in December 1945, and the Malay Nationalist Party (MNP) was founded a month earlier from the remnants of the pre-war, left-wing Kesatuan Melayu Muda, or KMM. At first the MDU and MNP took the position that Singapore could be merged with Malaya but by mid-1946, the Malay community had grown more nationalistic.

The Malayan Communist Party (MCP), the only organised Asian group to emerge intact from the Japanese occupation, had already been agitating both in Singapore and Malaya. By September 1945, the General Labour Union (GLU), a pre-war, pro-communist vehicle, was back in operation. The GLU staged numerous strikes culminating in a two-day general strike against the British Military Administration (BMA) in January 1946. That erupted when the GLU secretary-general was jailed by the BMA on charges of intimidation and extortion. The slowly reviving city suddenly ground to a halt with an estimated 173,000 employees stopping work. The BMA's decision to release the unionist convinced the communists that the BMA was weak and would take no action against them.

The MCP organised the Singapore Federation of Trade Unions (SFTU). At the peak of its power in mid-1947, two-thirds of Singapore's trade unions, representing 51,000 workers, were associated with the communists. Between 1945 and 1947, the SFTU organised 119 strikes. The MCP co-operated initially with the MDU on the issue of a self-governing united Malaya (including Singapore) within the British Commonwealth. However, riding the growing wave of Malay nationalism and seeing most of the strikes it had fostered failing, the communists grew frustrated and turned to even more radical actions.

Meanwhile, the behaviour of the British in post-war Singapore and throughout the region was often unhelpful and, if anything, encouraged political discontent. For example, the British planned to remove Malay sultans from their positions because they had allegedly co-operated with the Japanese. Sultan Ibrahim of Johore, in particular, was singled out. The British also forged ahead with the unpopular Malayan Union Scheme.

The October 1945 plan for a new constitution was a complicated process developed with input from the War Cabinet, the Malayan Planning Unit, the Colonial Office and the War Office. Instrumental throughout the process was Britain's head of the Eastern Colonial Department, Sir Edward Gent, who became the first governor of the Malayan Union.

Malays opposed the Union because they believed they would have a diminished role in the new more multi-racial society. The scheme increased Malay fears of Chinese domination, because for the first time, political rights on Malaya's non-Malay population would be conferred through the creation of a common citizenship. Dato Onn bin Ja'afar, a prominent Malay, formed the United Malays National Organisation (UMNO) in 1946, to resist the Malayan Union plan. Many within Singapore also opposed Gent's plan because they wanted to be part of Malaya.

Nevertheless, the British prevailed. On the last day of March 1946, the BMA stood down in favour of a civilian government, which succeeded it on the first day of April. The old Straits Settlements organisation was replaced with a constitutional reorganisation that involved both the Straits Settlement territories and the Federated and Unfederated Malay States. The new Crown Colonial government would now rule the nine Malay states, Penang and Malacca, with a separate government for Singapore. A special governor-general, later known as commissioner-general, was to oversee all British possessions and protectorates in the Far East. Self-government seemed to be ruled out for the Straits.

After the Malayan Union experiment failed in 1948, Gent was appointed High Commissioner to the newly created Federation of Malaya. Tragically, he died in a plane accident before returning to the United Kingdom.

Singapore, with a population of over 900,000, became a distinct and separate British colony, much like Hong Kong, ruled by a separate governor. Britain intended Singapore to be a free port, the headquarters of British commerce in the East and the bastion of a British defence system in Asia.

Unfortunately, the incoming administration was as colonially minded as the one that had existed before the war. This would prove its undoing, for Singapore and the Far East had changed irreversibly. Beneath Singapore's uneasy calm that posed as peace, ran escalating feelings of discontent and an urge for self-determination.

Tan Chin Tuan was thrust into this volatile situation. The banker was pulled into increased public service because of the need for leadership that could bridge the aspirations of Asians, with the controlling power still held by the British. Someone had to communicate between the two groups if there was to be orderly progress. Before Gent's untimely death, Colonial Secretary S.W. Jones had written him a letter, recommending TCT as the very person in Singapore the British could trust.

In 1945, TCT was appointed to the BMA Advisory Council. In 1946, when civil government was restored, the Governor's Advisory Council and Committee for the Reconstitution of the Singapore Legislative Council were formed. TCT was again appointed to both Councils. Governor Sir Franklin Gimson ran Singapore with the help of the Governor's Advisory Council till the introduction of the new constitution in 1948.

With civilian rule, the Legislative Council replaced the Advisory Council. In December 1947, the Governor appointed TCT a Justice of the Peace. On March 20, 1948, Tan Chin Tuan was nominated to the Legislative Council to represent the Singapore Chinese Chamber of Commerce as the unofficial member. He also served in another position of authority, as a member of the revived Executive Council.

Because of his influential standing in public life and at the OCBC, the new civilian government also sought TCT's advice on issues arising from the wartime use of Japanese currency. The Legislative Council appointed TCT to a committee to consider matters relating to bank deposits and loans made during the Occupation. Banks were technically liable for funds deposited and loaned in Japanese currency, even though that currency was now invalid and unsupported. The committee framed the Debtor and Creditor Ordinance, which settled who should pay whom and the amounts involved. The ordinance established relative values for Japanese currency vis-á-vis British funds for various times during the war and effectively settled the matter.

On the issue of independence, Tan Chin Tuan was opposed to the Malayan Union. TCT's predisposition toward autonomy had been growing for years. His early interest in independence stemmed from the mid-1930s, when he began to dream of a Singapore no longer subservient to the British, a place where citizens would be all treated equally and fairly, regardless of race.

However, TCT was also aware that an independent nation required trained and experienced administrators. He was mindful of Indonesia's experience, where junior administrative and sometimes even clerical staff, served in high office without being suitably trained. Singaporeans, he believed, did not yet have the education or the administrative experience and were thus unprepared at this time for independence.

His emerging position was one based on common sense and logic; independence for Singapore should only be achieved slowly and steadily. If the British withdrew immediately, there were few capable of taking over the helm. The British, despite their fallibility, still very much mattered during the transitional period. But, for the time being, he kept such views to himself.

TCT had reason to be cautious. The post-war British had little appetite for dissent. Stung by potent Indian nationalism during World War II, many colonial administrators were not about to entertain talk of political devolution in Singapore.

Indeed, many refused to see those born in Singapore as British subjects. TCT had risked his life battling that attitude in India, when he was ordered to register as an alien despite being a British subject. Now, home in Singapore, the issue reared its head. Many colonial officials considered Singapore-born Chinese, citizens of China. That policy had a dark side — the Banishment Ordinance, designed to keep the population in line. Trouble-making ethnic Chinese were exiled to China without trial. Similarly, ethnic Indians could be banished to India.

Tan Chin Tuan tactfully, and unofficially, spoke to Sir Franklin Charles Gimson on the issue. Gimson had been appointed governor and commander-in-chief of Singapore in 1946. TCT suggested that the new governor use the powers of the Banishment Ordinance very sparingly, to avoid inflaming the public. Gimson admired TCT's practical approach to such questions and would seek the banker's views when he had delicate issues to consider.

The British intransigence fostered a variety of hybrid political philosophies with differing intensities and fervours. Many of the leaders

Above: Tan Kah Kee, the powerful and influential leader of Singapore's Chinese community.

Chang Kia Ngau, general manager of the Bank of China.

The China Building in Singapore's Chulia Street.

*TCT in Australia, with his wife Helene and their children,
during the early days of World War II.*

In India, where OCBC relocated its operations during World War II.

TCT with Dato Onn bin Ja'afar (far left), leader of the United Malays National Organisation; and Malcolm MacDonald (second from left), commissioner-general in Southeast Asia.

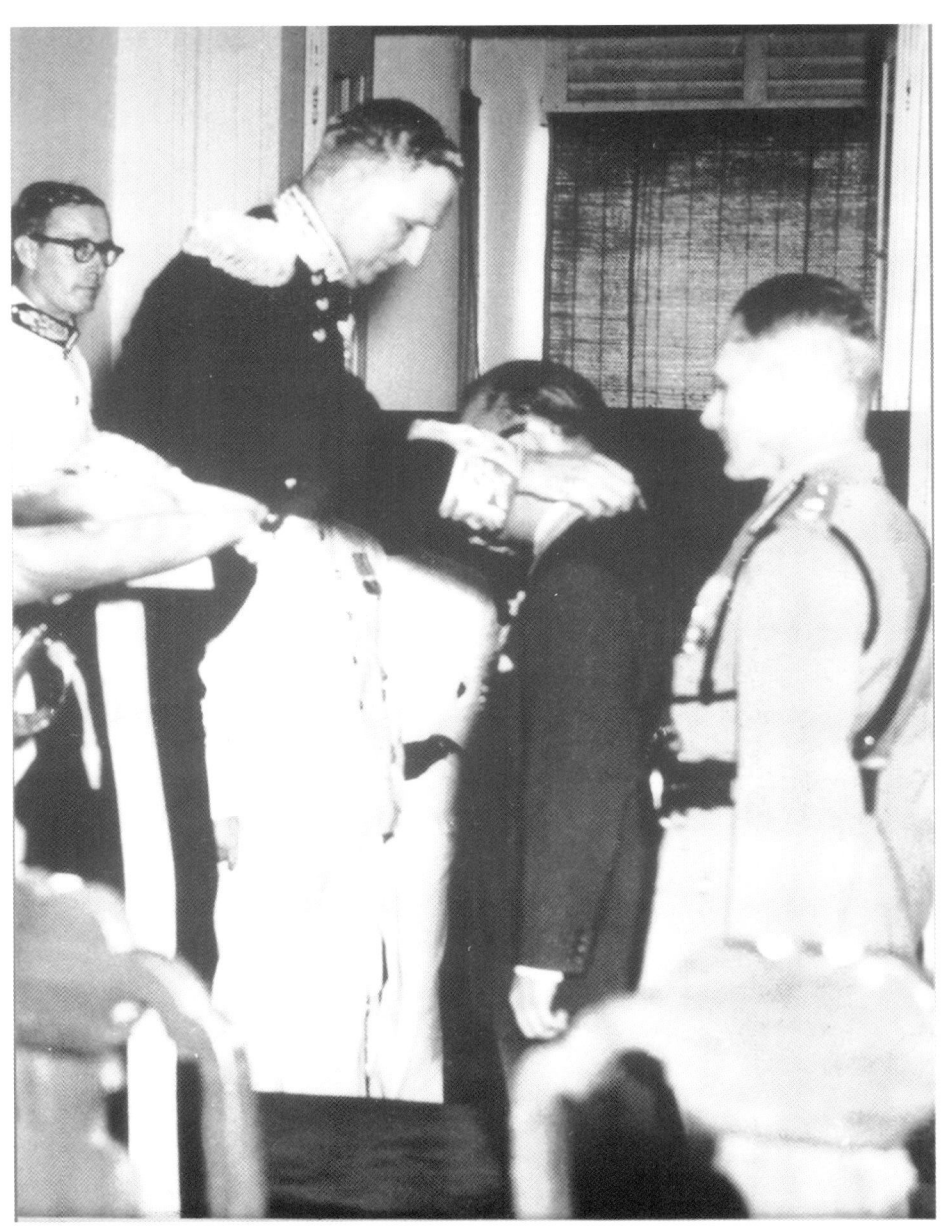

Receiving his CBE from Governor Sir Franklin Charles Gimson in 1951.

Taking the oath of deputy president of the Legislative Council.

Secretary of State for the Colonies Sir James Griffith discovers for himself TCT's legendary good taste in food.

The Duchess of Kent visits Singapore in 1952.

Sitting as a member of the Rendel Commission set up in 1953 to review Singapore's new constitution.

*Striking bank employees air their grievances outside the China
Building in the 1960s.*

Singapore's famous icon — The Raffles Hotel
Courtesy: National Archives of Singapore — James Song Collection

Robinson department store in Raffles Place. Courtesy: Robinson & Co

The Specialists' Centre on Orchard Road.

Touring the operations at Malayan Breweries.

*TCT celebrates fifty years of service with OCBC and
its predecessor bank in 1975.*

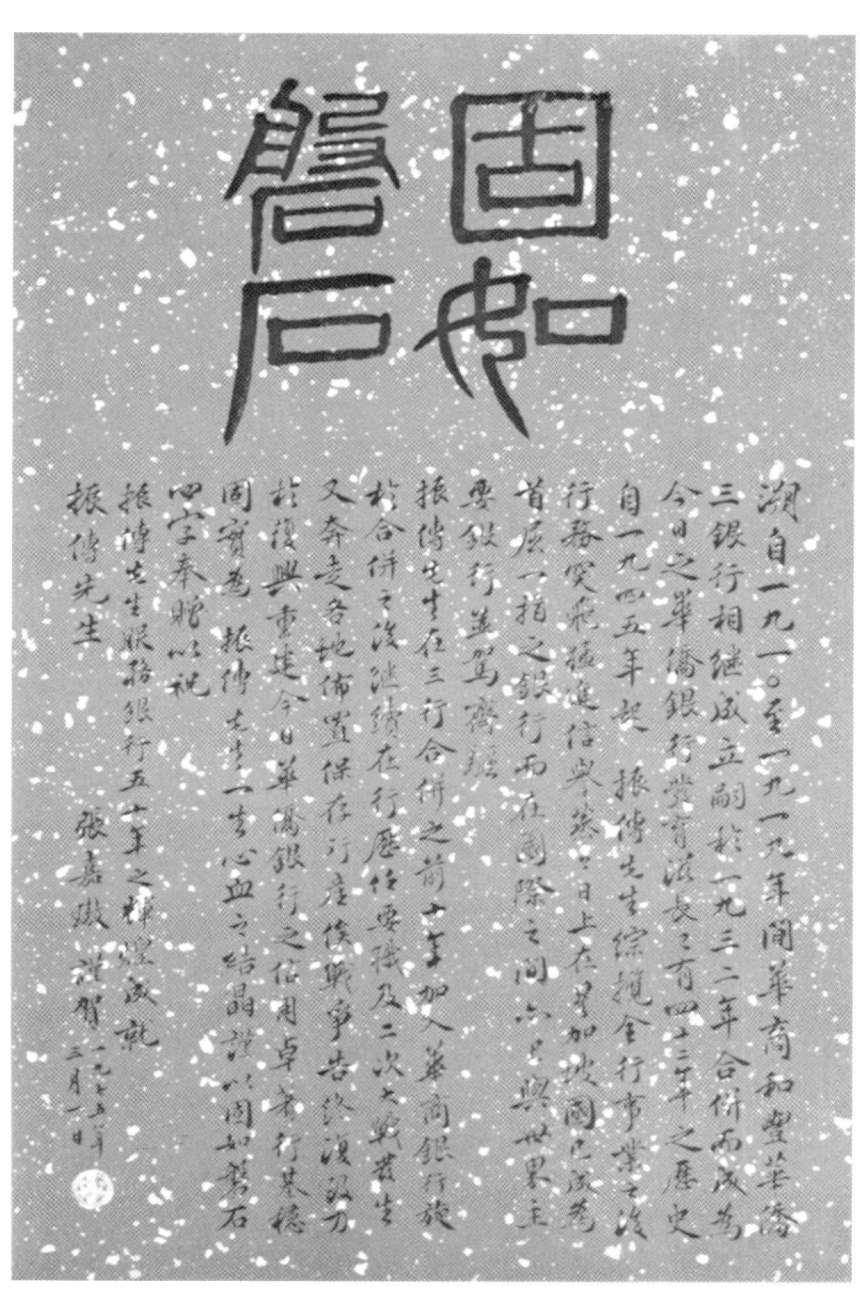

Chang Kia Ngau's scroll for TCT's fiftieth anniversary celebrations.

Construction of the OCBC Centre begins.

Singapore's skyline alters as the OCBC Centre moves higher.

*Celebrations in the banking hall at the opening of
the OCBC Centre in 1976.*

Receiving an honorary degree from Singapore president and National University of Singapore chancellor Wee Kim Wee in 1991.

of these embryonic movements eventually sought TCT's advice and counsel. Even Dato Onn bin Ja'afar came from his home in Johore to enlist TCT's assistance for his UMNO party's protest against the Malayan Union scheme.

Using tact and diplomacy, Tan Chin Tuan managed to successfully straddle Singapore's two isolated communities. Not only was he a well-connected conduit to the Chinese, he was also someone who had maintained impeccable credentials as a loyal British subject. His candour and bluntness were mixed with considerable charm, faultless manners and a sense of humour. The British enjoyed dealing with TCT and in most cases, respected his opinion.

The British were so eager to proceed with the Malayan Union that they not only disregarded his recommendations, but also those of all the dissenting leaders on both sides of the Causeway. TCT had a protest letter endorsed by more than 200 Chinese organisations representing 300,000 Chinese residents in the colony, but the British ignored their request.

TCT believed Singapore's future was at stake. As a nominated official, he could not openly support the nationalists, but he quietly sympathised with the organisers of a protest against federation. It was planned by a number of groups, including the All-Malaya Council of Joint Action (AMCJA) and the Pusat-Tenaga Ra'ayat (PUTERA). Tan Chin Tuan advised against demonstrations and instead supported the idea of a one-day *hartal* (peaceful work stoppage), which would serve to paralyse the nation without risking violent response from the authorities. Even the Singapore Chinese Chamber of Commerce backed the group action. It had called for equal representation in the legislature for Malays and Chinese and equal rights for all citizens and wanted to restrict the veto powers of the British High Commissioner. But these voices fell on deaf ears.

The *hartal*, staged on October 20, 1947, was obvious and meaningful — and remained non-violent. The country literally came to a standstill

— even rickshaw pullers stayed off the street. However, the broad coalition that worked together for the *hartal* was to fall apart within a year. Tan Chin Tuan, and the Chinese Chamber of Commerce that had backed the strike, withdrew from the AMCJA-PUTERA movement, while the communists departed to embark on a policy of armed insurrection in Malaya, which was to have far-reaching consequences.

Fortunately for Singapore, a new breed of British administrator arrived from London, less colonial-minded and more open to the prospect of Asian self-determination. He was Malcolm MacDonald, an Oxford-trained member of parliament, who had served the British government extensively, including the assignment of secretary of state for the dominions in the mid-1930s. This well-qualified man was appointed governor-general of the Malayan Union in 1946.

The son of Great Britain's first Labour prime minister, Ramsay MacDonald, Malcolm MacDonald was an astute choice. MacDonald would govern wisely for two years, until his diplomatic career advanced further with his appointment as commissioner-general for the United Kingdom in Southeast Asia.

TCT grew to know and respect MacDonald, frequently spending weekends at his private residence and dining out with him. The two men appreciated each other. Like TCT, he was democratic, recognising all men were equal, regardless of their racial origins. However much this liberal attitude might have rankled the old colonial hands, it was clear that MacDonald's friendship with Tan Chin Tuan represented the future for all Singapore.

MacDonald worked in co-operation with Singapore's new governor and commander-in-chief, Sir Franklin Gimson. An astute and experienced administrator, Gimson had spent World War II in a civilian prison camp in Hong Kong. Almost singled-handedly, he reasserted Britain's claim to that colony in the political vacuum following Japanese surrender. It was considered an audacious and decisive move. TCT was to grow exceedingly fond of Gimson during the years he served in Singapore. The governor was so respected that after his retirement, TCT held a subscription drive to pay for a portrait of Gimson to hang in the municipal buildings. The initiative raised 50 per cent more than was required.

Despite the rapport between these high-ranking officials and the banker, bigotry continued to thrive within the colonial community. One evening, Gimson invited Tan Chin Tuan and the Chinese Consul General, Wu Pak Shing, for dinner. After the meal, an aide-de-camp courteously reminded the governor that he had been invited to attend a special function that evening at the Tanglin Club, an exclusive, whites-only British haunt. As Gimson was invited as the guest-of-honour, he asked TCT and the consul general to accompany him. Soon thereafter, a club executive wrote to the governor to point out that the rules of the Club had been infringed by the attendance of the two Asians.

When Malcolm MacDonald heard about this affront to his friend, the governor-general demonstrated his contempt for hidebound British custom by boycotting the Tanglin Club, as well as the Singapore Golf Club, which also forbade Asians access.

Instead, MacDonald joined the Island Club, which welcomed people of all races. In 1949, Tan Chin Tuan served as its president, running for the position against a European director of Sime Darby.

Later, Tan Chin Tuan would stand down as president of the Island Club in favour of Malcolm MacDonald. The governor-general, for his part, obtained Royal patronage for the club, so it became known as the Royal Island Club, a powerful and appropriate snub to the racists at the Tanglin. Eventually, the Tanglin Club amended its rules. Although Tan Chin Tuan could have joined the Club, he declined.

However, as honourable as the governor and governor-general were, they were still obliged to obey orders from London. Following the 1947 *hartal*, increasing communist infiltration and escalating violence would prompt the British to declare a state of emergency in Malaya and

Singapore, which would last from 1948 until 1960.

The British were caught off guard by the degree to which the communists had grown active. They failed to see that their resistance fighting against the Japanese had made the communists appear heroic in the eyes of many people on the Malay Peninsula. The British announced a draconian series of powers, the Emergency Regulations, which saw more than 1,200 people detained in Singapore alone.

The regulations were intended to fight the communist insurgency, but they failed to stop a number of violent acts, including an unsuccessful attempt to assassinate Governor Gimson at the Happy World Stadium and the burning down of the Aik Ho Rubber Factory in Johore.

Anti-British feelings were running high. It was a time for sensible men to seek justice, to take the path of reason and negotiation and to bring calm to the hysteria. For example, in 1951, the British detained a man named Lee Seng Peng and accused him of yielding to communist extortion.

The British authorities alleged that Lee Seng Peng had arranged for the payment of $30,000 to a terrorist agent. TCT believed that Lee, who was employed by the Malayan rubber baron Lee Kong Chian, was being held unjustly and considered the evidence against the man flimsy. There was no direct proof that the communists' extortion note was even delivered to the accused man, nor was there any indication that Lee paid the funds. The British were relying on the allegations of certain questionable individuals, including a captured communist guerrilla. Lee Seng Peng, who was suffering from tuberculosis, was held in custody in squalid conditions, without bail or proper charges being laid. Although he had never met the man, Tan Chin Tuan took up his cause.

TCT wrote to Colonel Henry Lee Hau-Shik in February 1951 and asked the member of the Federal Council to look into the matter:

> "It seems to me that Government is being unnecessarily oppressive towards innocent members of our community. No one can object to its being tough with the guilty, but we expect in Malaya British and democratic-like treatment of those not found guilty."

TCT's intercession angered a powerful British military officer, General Gerald Templer, the man in charge of administering the Emergency Regulations. Few dared to oppose Templer. Colonel Lee passed a copy of TCT's letter to Templer, infuriating the general. In the end, Templer ordered the detained Lee Seng Peng freed, but used the case to take issue with the banker from Singapore.

Templer arranged for Governor Gimson to invite Tan Chin Tuan to tea. TCT was astonished when he entered the parlour and encountered the General. After introductions and a smattering of polite conversation, Gimson tactfully withdrew, leaving the two men alone. "You criticised me," Templer complained, "You wrote to H.S. Lee." TCT countered that his action was not criticism, but an honest opinion on how the Malayan government had acted too drastically. Templer was a tough but reasonable man and he listened to Tan Chin Tuan's rationale — how he always sought to champion the cause of democratic rights.

After hearing TCT's analysis and recognising that his actions were in the pure pursuit of justice, Templer extended his hand in a gentlemanly gesture. He expressed his appreciation that TCT had acted tactfully and behind the scenes, instead of running to the newspapers, stirring up public discord. The meeting concluded with Templer recommending, "In future, if you have any matter of importance, address them to me directly."

On one occasion in Tan Chin Tuan's home, Lady Keightley, a friend of Lady Templer, was enchanted by one of the banker's birds, a handsome white cockatoo that strutted about the sitting room and haughtily climbed up TCT's trouser leg. Lady Templer heard about it and subsequently wrote to Tan Chin Tuan inquiring where she could get a bird like that. Tan Chin Tuan offered to find one for her and when he secured it, he had the cockatoo air-freighted to Kuala Lumpur. Lady Templer personally went to the airport in her limousine to receive the precious parrot, which was eventually named *Chao Nao*, or "Noisy".

Her staff was surprised — they thought she had driven to the airport to meet a dignitary!

Tan Chin Tuan enjoys presenting thoughtful gifts to his friends. He even gave his own cockatoo, which was tame and talkative, to the Sultan of Johore, Sir Ismail Tungku Mahkota, in honour of their close and cordial friendship.

However, although Tan Chin Tuan and General Templer became firm friends, it did not stop them from having disagreements. For example, TCT was a member of the Malayan Singapore Liaison Committee. But he and the committee failed to prevent the general from rounding up ethnic Chinese squatters and putting them into "settlements". In the Malayan government's attempt to prevent the communists from acquiring supplies, the people lost their farms and livestock. To deny the enemy, innocent people suffered.

The army ignored all criticisms of their actions, even when it came from as eminent a personage as Tan Kah Kee. Instead, the British accused him of being pro-communist and instructed the Singapore government to detain him. Tan Chin Tuan immediately stepped in to support this great man. He argued that Tan Kah Kee had done nothing wrong in Singapore and threatened to speak out publicly on Tan Kah Kee's behalf.

Governor-General MacDonald listened to Tan Chin Tuan and then advised the Singapore governor that Tan Kah Kee should not be held. The extradition order was rescinded, but TCT counselled Tan Kah Kee not to cross the Straits of Johore and risk detention in Malaya. Eventually, the man admired by all Singapore Chinese grew weary of peninsular intrigue and abandoned the region. He initially considered going to Taiwan, but he had grown disaffected with the corruption of the Kuomintang government there. His sympathies grew for Mao Zedong. In the end, Tan Kah Kee relocated to southeast China, to help further education in the community. Singapore lost a great man and TCT lost a good friend.

Although self-government was not proceeding as quickly as some would have liked, the British were not unopposed to the concept. Indeed, in March 1948, they had given the people in Singapore a taste of democracy by holding the first-ever elections for six of the twenty-two seats on the Legislative Council. TCT's seat, however, remained an appointed position. The British decision to hold partial elections corresponded with Tan Chin Tuan's position on slow and gradual devolution of power to the locals. Three lawyers — C.C. Tan, N.A. Mallal and TCT's old friend John Laycock — formed a group known as the Singapore Progressive Party in August 1947.

Like TCT, the party was devoted to gradual self-government. Although TCT shunned party politics, the Progressives eagerly courted his support. When the election was held, only a small number of Singapore residents were registered to vote. The Progressives took half of the six elected seats and were to dominate Singapore party politics until 1955.

Throughout this period, Tan Chin Tuan maintained a hectic and accelerating pace with his business enterprises. Apart from serving as managing director at the OCBC, he was now involved in other corporations as well. In 1950, he accepted directorships of three Singapore companies in which the OCBC had shareholdings: Fraser and Neave Ltd, a bottler of soft drinks; Raffles Hotel Ltd; and Robinson & Company Ltd, a retail department store. The following year he was appointed to the board of Malayan Breweries Ltd and became deputy chairman of The Overseas Assurance Corp Ltd. In 1954, he took on additional duties as a director for The Straits Trading Company Ltd, a renowned miner of tin — the first Chinese ever to serve on its board.

But these appointments meant long and hard hours. It took remarkable stamina and a quick, organised mind to endure this gruelling pace. At the height of his political career during the decade following the Japanese defeat, he would work a full day at the bank and the other businesses, and then go directly to government meetings, which often lasted until midnight or one in the morning. When there were no meetings, there were the essential rounds of social occasions, sometimes three in one evening, which lubricated political co-operation. And there were speeches to write. Still mindful of the humiliation he had endured when he first addressed the municipal council in 1939, Tan Chin Tuan took great pains to ensure his speeches were grammatically perfect, erudite and convincing.

TCT's public service had not gone unnoticed. As he was exceedingly well connected to influential people in both the Chinese and British communities of Singapore, he became the conduit between the two. His steadily widening network of friends and allies helped to advance one another's common beliefs.

Even Buckingham Palace came to recognise his leadership and efforts on behalf of Singapore. On January 1, 1951, Tan Chin Tuan was honoured with a Commander of the Most Excellent Order of the British Empire (Civil Division). The CBE was awarded for his distinguished and meritorious public service. Typically, Tan Chin Tuan was unable to travel to London to receive this honour, for he was too busy with his responsibilities to the bank and to Singapore. In the months to come, he would become even busier. Governor Gimson had an important job for Tan Chin Tuan.

Growing Unrest, Declining Colonialism

In April 1951, Governor Sir Franklin Gimson informed Tan Chin Tuan that he was creating a new position for him within the Legislative Council, that of deputy president. The appointment meant that, after the governor, he would be second in protocol in Singapore, the first Asian to achieve this distinction.

Gimson's confidence and trust in TCT dated back to 1947 on the occasion when the governor had exercised his casting vote and sanctioned the introduction of income tax — in the face of unanimous opposition from the unofficials led by Tan Chin Tuan and C.C. Tan, who both resigned from the Advisory Council on that account.

Recognising the intensity of the opposition towards his veto, the governor urged the two men to withdraw their resignations. He even extended an invitation to TCT to return to the council, not once but twice. Tan Chin Tuan finally did so after much persuasion but on the condition that the governor undertook not to exercise his veto power again in future.

Tan Chin Tuan secured that concession, an achievement which C.C. Tan attributed to Tan Chin Tuan's ability to raise the status of the council above that of a rubber-stamp of the British policy-makers.

That episode left a deep impression on Gimson. The governor sensed the need for change and took appropriate steps to appoint Tan Chin Tuan deputy president of the legislature and to function as its de facto chairman.

In a letter, Gimson wrote that he hoped "your office to be regarded as one with definite duties and functions and not as a mere position of distinction that carried no responsibility." Added to his obligations to the Legislative and Executive councils, TCT, at the age of only forty-three, had become the most important Asian in Singapore's government.

The appointment was to put him in the centre of the day-to-day action in the Legislative Council. Frequently he chaired proceedings because the governor, as president of the council, did not always attend. A *Sunday Times* feature writer, reporting on the selection, described TCT as "the most obvious choice".

Gimson chose Tan Chin Tuan for the position for four important reasons. TCT had long experience serving on the council and on many government committees and private corporations, so the British were comfortable entrusting him with chairing the Legislative Council. TCT had the support of the Chinese community. His political skills were based on a deep belief in fairness, justice and equality. Finally, his social skills and his kindness were disarming. He had few equals on the island of Singapore and as his personal currency grew with all whom he met, his power increased correspondingly.

His access to high places widened significantly beyond the borders of the Malay Peninsula. Tan Chin Tuan's charm and thoughtfulness naturally built an intricate network of influential friends. He was always there to help them and they often reciprocated. For example, during some of the numerous trips to London TCT made on behalf of the bank, he became friends with the Secretary of State for the Colonies, A.T. Lennox-Boyd. The Secretary of State determined policy for dependent territories of the Commonwealth and thus exerted enormous power. Singapore's governor and governor-general would be obliged to enforce policies forged in England. The relationship between TCT and Lennox-Boyd was so warm that even Governor Gimson was once kept waiting in an antechamber whilst Tan Chin Tuan was ushered in to see the

Secretary of State. Later in his career, as head of the famed Irish brewery Guinness, Lennox-Boyd would continue to call on TCT when he visited Singapore on business.

Lennox-Boyd's successor, Sir James Griffith, also became a good friend and powerful ally. During a tour of Singapore, TCT, hosted the new secretary of state to a sumptuous Chinese meal. Tan Chin Tuan is a lifelong gourmet and his taste in good food is legendary. When the banker visited the Colonial Secretary in London on another occasion, Sir James reminisced about the meal and wished out loud that he could find one as delicious in England.

Responding to that, TCT set about arranging a special Chinese meal in the British capital. He knew a man from China named Kwok, who owned the Asiatic Restaurant in London. Kwok had originally served as secretary of the Chinese embassy in London, but after the communist revolution of 1949, he no longer wished to continue in his government's service. Instead, he opened a restaurant.

TCT first discovered the Asiatic when a group of students had taken him there. Upon returning on his own, Kwok told TCT, "I'm sorry but I cannot charge you the same price as the students paid last time. They have no money, so I charge them less, but I have to charge you according to the menu." This generosity towards the impoverished students greatly impressed Tan Chin Tuan. He also learned that Kwok had to buy his Chinese food ingredients directly from Hong Kong, since there were no suppliers in the United Kingdom who could provide them at an affordable price. Unfortunately, even the Hong Kong suppliers were expensive, depriving Kwok of the opportunity to improve his business.

To help the restaurateur, TCT approached Kwok's banker, the Midland Bank, and asked his colleagues there to extend a letter of credit to Kwok for 2,000 pounds sterling to allow him to build his business. The surprised Kwok was so grateful that when TCT wished to host a meal for Sir James Griffith, Kwok actually went to the Chinese embassy and borrowed their best cook. Sir James was delighted with the meal and the restaurateur was pleased to have helped.

Tan Chin Tuan had a way of impressing even the most important dignitaries. When the Duchess of Kent was due in Singapore on an official visit in 1952, the new governor, Sir John Nicoll, preoccupied with ceremony, informed the unofficial members of the Legislative and Executive councils that they could arrange a dinner in her honour provided they all wore coat tails. The unofficials were opposed to a formal banquet, because they would have to go to the expense and trouble of having formal wear made for a one-time use only. They suggested mess jackets instead. But the governor would not be moved on this issue of protocol.

During a meeting with the Duchess's private secretary to finalise arrangements, TCT pleaded the unofficials' case. Soon the governor received a communication from the Duchess, stating: "Her Royal Highness commands that there shall be no tails." The visit proved a success.

When the Duchess inspected the troops based in Singapore, TCT quietly suggested that instead of the regal isolation of a Rolls-Royce, the Duchess might wish to ride in an open jeep. Again, the Duchess readily agreed, to the delight of those who now had an unobstructed view of royalty.

On another occasion during the same visit, TCT invited Governor-General Malcolm MacDonald and the Duchess of Kent to dinner at Bedok. The Duchess enjoyed the local ambience and the informality of the occasion, although Governor Nicoll was less enthusiastic, thinking it unseemly. He frowned on the lowly food hawkers lining the pavement, hardly suitable company, in Nicoll's mind, for nobility. But the Duchess, known for being both unpretentious and gregarious, found Bedok fascinating. She sampled a variety of dishes from several stalls. After her visit, one or two enterprising hawkers put up a sign, which grandly stated, "By Royal Patronage".

It was important for those born in Singapore like TCT to exercise their influence with the British prudently, without any sign of unction that would degrade their fellow Asians. When in 1952, London asked for funds from its colonies and protectorates to pay for the costs of the war effort, the issue met with resistance in the Legislative Council. "Why should we give them funds?" grumbled one Chinese councillor, "They failed to protect us." But TCT took up the subject. As he stood in the legislature on December 16th, to make the motion, Tan Chin Tuan eloquently compared the sacrifices the peoples of Britain had made, and were continuing to make, to the current surpluses Singapore was enjoying:

> "I rise to move the motion standing in my name, that this Council approves a special defence contribution of $8,570,000 to her Majesty's Government as a mark of loyalty of the Government and people of Singapore and of their determination to assist Her Majesty's Government to bear the heavy burden of the defence programme.

> "We in Singapore have benefited by all these preparatory measures to defend our freedom, and as during the last few years, for example in 1950 and 1951, the Colony has had surpluses of $16.9 million and $53 million respectively, it seems to me only fair and appropriate that Singapore should in some way show its appreciation of the difficulties which Her Majesty's Government is facing and of the determined and costly efforts which she is and has been making and of our determination to stand by her by making at this time a special defence contribution of $8,570,000, this being roughly equal to one million pounds sterling... Our gift is such a small drop in the mighty ocean of expense incurred by Her Majesty's Government that if it could be made without any sacrifice on our part, it would be worth little."

> — Second session of Second Legislative Council
> December 16, 1952

Despite initial opposition in the council, the articulate logic convinced the dissenters. Amid enthusiastic applause, the motion was carried.

Tan Chin Tuan's lifelong pursuit of justice was based on his fervent belief in equality and fairness. To him, personalities were secondary. It was not uncommon for TCT to intervene to help those he had never met, or even those who had crossed swords with him. In one such instance, he heard of the plight of Police Superintendent W.R.M. Haxworth, a man he disliked. The British-born Haxworth had been found guilty of indiscipline following a speech he had given to the Rotary Club, complaining that the government hadn't provided him with sufficient resources for his men to do their duty.

TCT had previously had an unhappy personal encounter with the pompous traffic police superintendent. Haxworth had stopped Tan Chin Tuan's car at the Esplanade, demanding to see his identity card. Although both men knew each other, Haxworth insisted on inspecting TCT's papers. Believing the request to be ludicrous and the man officious, TCT refused. Tan Chin Tuan observed that power had a habit of going to men's heads, especially those with an arrogant bent like Haxworth. So he took his objections to the Commissioner of Police.

Commissioner R.E. Foulger supported Haxworth. "He was doing his duty," Foulger told TCT. "You shouldn't have refused."

TCT pressed Foulger further. "Does it mean when he sees you, he must see your identity card?"

"Certainly," replied Foulger.

"Don't be ridiculous," TCT replied.

But this incident did not prevent Tan Chin Tuan from later helping Haxworth when his speech to the Rotarians aroused official ire and he was threatened with dismissal. A decidedly humbler Haxworth approached TCT. "Sir," he pleaded. "I have 32 years service. I'll lose my pension. I'm told you are the only one who can help."

TCT asked if he had appealed to the Police Commissioner. Haxworth replied that he had, but nothing had come of it.

"I'll see what I can do about it," TCT said finally.

Tan Chin Tuan decided to bring the matter up to Governor Sir John Nicoll.

"Why are you always interfering with my people?" the governor grumbled, "He's a Britisher."

"I'm a Britisher too," Tan Chin Tuan reminded Nicoll, before returning to the subject of Haxworth. "Please temper justice with mercy."

"Are you trying to teach me?" Nicoll responded testily.

"No, I am merely asking you to reconsider."

Nicoll was unmoved. "I must administer the punishment."

"Then Sir," said TCT, choosing his words carefully, "I hope you will allow me to plead this case at the Legislative Council. You have the right to ignore me, but I also have the right to make the plea to you publicly, in the open. Let our learned councillors be the judge."

Airing the matter before the legislature was not in Nicoll's best interest. Council meetings were regularly reported back to the House of Commons in England. The governor was aware that TCT was friendly with several MPs in the UK including the Secretary of State. Should Haxworth's situation reach the ears of a sympathetic MP who might take up his cause, it would not benefit Nicoll's career.

The following day TCT received a telephone call from Governor Nicoll advising that he had changed his mind and decided to spare Haxworth from outright dismissal. Instead, Haxworth was given a reprimand and eventually allowed to retire from the force with his pension intact.

Throughout his career, TCT was willing to fight injustice or right a wrong on behalf of another. When others were silent, he spoke out. When others stood passively by, he acted.

One stranger who benefited from Tan Chin Tuan's acute sense of justice and fairness was Wong Lai Fatt, a Malaysian vegetable seller. While reading the paper one morning in October 1972, TCT came across the story about Wong who had pleaded guilty to killing a loan shark, Cheng Peng Fun.

Cheng had forced Wong's wife into several acts of prostitution to recover $120 which Wong owed him. Even after the debt had been repaid, Cheng wanted Wong's wife to continue to earn money for him. Accompanied by two men, Cheng went to Wong's house to proposition

Wong's wife and, in Wong's presence, tried to rape her. In desperation, Wong stabbed Cheng with a kitchen knife, killing him.

Although Wong was a complete stranger, Tan Chin Tuan felt compassion for the man and his desperate situation. He contacted R.C. Hoffman, managing partner of the Kuala Lumpur firm of Allen & Gledhill to appeal the case. "If the report is accurate, I think you will agree with me that the defendant was apparently trying to defend his wife from being raped by a scoundrel who had driven them into ignominy, and the four-year prison sentence is unwarranted."

The case was a difficult one. Wong had pleaded guilty and his conviction was not appealed. Furthermore, the time for lodging an appeal had passed. On TCT's insistence, Hoffman brought the case to the personal attention of Malaysia's Chief Justice, Tan Sri Ong Hock Thye, who allowed an appeal to be filed out of time. On appeal, the three-man Federal Court quashed Wong's conviction.

Afterwards, in a letter to TCT, Chief Justice Ong Hock Thye wrote:

"I am much obliged to you for calling my attention last month to the case of Wong Lai Fatt, which escaped my attention altogether when it was reported. I am more than grateful to you in that you have, in spite of being such a very busy man, not been content just to say, 'What a pity' and left it at that."

TCT responded:

"It has made me very happy to see this miscarriage of justice so mercifully rectified, although I neither know nor have ever set eyes on the defendant."

A profoundly grateful Wong wrote to Tan Chin Tuan.

"Due to my having received not much education, I am unable to use all the words to express the deep gratitude in my heart for your kind deed. All I can do is to say 'thanks' and give my respect to you and to all philanthropists who have bestowed kindness on others without expecting to be rewarded. May I extend my best and sincere wishes to you and to all beneficent people. May all of us with a kind heart be rewarded by their good deeds."

Another who benefited from TCT's intervention was the renowned surgeon, Professor Yeoh Ghim Seng. The English-trained doctor had been a war hero, perfecting his surgical skills on British troops injured in battle.

After World War II, Dr Yeoh returned to Singapore and joined a hospital to continue his practice. However, he met with stiff resistance from the colonial doctors, who were only willing to accept him in the subservient role as their assistant. Dr Yeoh tried without success to secure a quota of hospital beds, which would enable him to operate on patients as a full-fledged surgeon.

When Yeoh complained to a senior surgeon, the British doctor issued an arrogant challenge — they would both perform appendectomies at the same time, so the hospital could assess Yeoh's speed and skill. The "competition" was held when two suitable patients became available. The British surgeon was only partially through his operation when Yeoh entered the room, declaring that he had finished. Instead of proffering the deserved apology, the colonial surgeon handed instruments to Dr Yeoh and got him to assist him like a surgical nurse, while the European completed the operation.

Some time later, when the doctor and his wife were playing tennis with TCT, Professor Yeoh disclosed that he was leaving Singapore for Hong Kong. When asked why, the surgeon reluctantly related his story. Tan Chin Tuan immediately took action by addressing Governor Nicoll on the issue. Initially, the Governor insisted that his hands were tied, as it was a matter for the Colonial Medical Service. In response, TCT calmly declared he would raise the matter in a session of the Legislative Council.

Considerations like those in the Haxworth case led the Governor to decide in the end to speak to the director of medical services and Yeoh Ghim Seng was granted the beds to which he was entitled. TCT's intervention assured that Singapore benefited from the skilful hands of this eminent surgeon.

TCT was never reckless in his causes. He took calculated risks, using decorum and courtesy. But he was also a born fighter, who would never compromise his principles and would courageously attempt to correct a wrong. He lived his life combining pragmatism, common sense and grace, summed up in a favourite slogan, "Forbear, forgive and forget."

Tan Chin Tuan's desire for a positive relationship among equals was personified in his friendship with Malcolm MacDonald. Unlike the rigid and class-conscious Governor Nicoll, MacDonald represented the new, enlightened European in Singapore. Well-versed in Asian matters and with close links to the decision-makers in the British government, MacDonald now served as commissioner-general for Malaya and Singapore. Although MacDonald took precedence over Nicoll, the governor frequently took issue with his status at ceremonial occasions, such as the Queen's Birthday. Ever gracious, MacDonald was not obsessed with rank, being more concerned with good government and dealing fairly with people.

MacDonald saw his Asian friends as full partners in building post-war Singapore. TCT was a regular guest in the MacDonalds' home and retreat at Bukit Serene. Their friendship also symbolised the future of Singapore — racial harmony and co-operation, and a vivacity that makes the modern city-state unique in Southeast Asia.

MacDonald was a high-spirited man who loved life in the Orient. His informality contrasted sharply with Nicoll's haughtiness. After Governor Gimson had chosen Tan Chin Tuan to lead the Legislative Council, his successor, Governor Nicoll, declared that even though TCT was deputy president, he would not be called chairman of the proceedings. Technically, insisted Governor Nicoll, only the governor could be the president of Legco, despite the fact that TCT effectively ran the chamber.

One evening, TCT took MacDonald down to Keong Saik Road. They visited a restaurant run by a man named Chiew Kee, a racehorse owner renowned for his Cantonese cuisine. Unfortunately, the street also had another reputation — the concubines, who were kept there by wealthy men.

The unpretentious MacDonald not only eschewed stuffy Colonial Service protocol, but that night he also dodged his personal bodyguards. Keong Saik Road was swirling with people dining, drinking and carousing. It was a security man's nightmare, an uncontrollable situation where MacDonald's life could be jeopardised in the blink of an eye. These thoughts played on TCT's mind and he became concerned. Quietly, he telephoned the police to inform them that MacDonald was without security. Before long, a tall, burly European appeared opposite Chiew Kee's shop — the assistant commissioner of police himself. While they were eating, MacDonald looked up and noticed him. "Why the devil did he come?" he complained, obviously annoyed by the official intrusion. Tan Chin Tuan said nothing.

When they emerged after their meal, the two men were astonished to find the busy street had emptied. The police had set up cars at either end of the block. Fearing there was going to be a vice-squad raid, the men who frequented the street to visit their concubines fled the area. MacDonald was highly amused by the incident and fondly recalled it in his memoirs.

Between the years 1951 and 1955, a quickening pace of events would lead to partial self-government for Singapore. Tan Chin Tuan's political career accelerated correspondingly. It would be a time when he would have to draw on all his skills and energy to deal with the complex challenges facing Singapore and Malaya.

Tan Chin Tuan's negotiation and conciliation talents were put to the test during a particularly difficult strike. There had been several work stoppages after the war, partly due to political agitation by communists, and partly due to genuine labour disputes. One of the worst post-war strikes to afflict Singapore was the postal walkout of

February 1952, the first post-war confrontation by a government trade union. Five hundred postmen and telegraph messengers walked off the job, when the government failed to reach a collective agreement with the workers' union. Despite extended negotiations between seven union leaders and three officials representing the government, the controller of labour reported a stalemate to the Executive Council. "Why can we not settle this deadlock?" TCT wondered aloud in the council meeting. The governor turned to him and asked: "Would you like to try to settle it?" TCT agreed to try.

Armed with a mandate from the government, Tan Chin Tuan called Lee Kuan Yew, a young lawyer and political activist, from the firm of Laycock & Ong. Lee was representing the Postal and Telecommunication Uniformed Staff Union and would later become Singapore's first prime minister. The two men are related through marriage — Lee Kuan Yew is married to TCT's niece, the daughter of his wife's sister. Their children played together in the banker's home every week. The family relationship was conducive to a less formal approach. TCT picked up the phone and called the lawyer, asking cordially, "Harry (as he was known in private), can we not settle this postal strike?"

Tan Chin Tuan then visited Lee Kuan Yew's office for a private meeting. The next day, both men arranged for the union's president, secretary and a few others to meet at TCT's office at OCBC. Tan Chin Tuan served cakes and tea, a small but gracious gesture contributing toward a non-combative atmosphere. On behalf of the government, he made some concessions, and the union reciprocated with their own compromises. The negotiations took time, as proposals went back and forth between the government and the union leadership, but by working quietly behind the scenes, the thirteen-day strike was ultimately settled.

The Governor was so delighted he invited TCT to spend the day with him on St. John's Island, off Singapore's coast. But just before he was to leave for the outing, TCT received a telephone call from Lee

Kuan Yew who, addressing him as "*Emtio* (uncle)", sought his assistance to resolve some problems connected with the negotiations. TCT went to the union hall in Maxwell Road and addressed a rank and file meeting, which had been called to ratify the agreement. Some of the members were not yet convinced of the deal's soundness. Tan Chin Tuan gave an honest appraisal of how each side benefited. The postal workers reconsidered and the issue was resolved.

Singapore was becoming restless and potentially hostage to unions, communists, strikes and riots. TCT believed that it was essential to have a top-notch police force to control any potential disorder. His work on the Police Pay Code Committee increased the numbers and commitment of the Singapore police force. The security of the city was also strengthened by his convincing the government to adopt the then innovative use of radio-dispatched patrol cars, which made police work more efficient and responsive.

The decade after the war saw TCT working at a pace which few men could sustain or possibly imagine. Between 1948 and 1955, Tan Chin Tuan served on more than three-dozen official committees on the First and Second Legislative councils. The appointments covered a range of issues: financial matters, such as income tax and life insurance; real estate planning, such as rent control and land acquisition; and regulatory concerns, such as deportation and immigration control. In addition, the deputy president participated in a number of unrecorded critical situations, working quietly behind the scenes.

But the most far-reaching work that Tan Chin Tuan did during those years of public service was his contribution to the Rendel Commission. This committee, appointed by the government in July 1953, sought to review Singapore's constitution with an eye toward autonomy.

Chaired by Sir George Rendel, a notable ambassador, the nine-man commission was made up of the Attorney-General, the president of the City Council, plus important representatives of the Chinese, Indian and

Malay communities. TCT's co-panellists were eager for full and quick independence, but in long meetings that stretched from 5 P.M. until midnight, Tan Chin Tuan argued for his vision of a gradual and stable transition.

The commission finally reported to London in late winter of the following year, calling for significant changes. TCT would have preferred more time to consider all the ramifications of the recommendations, but Sir George urged the panel to hasten its deliberations, as he was obliged to return to England for the impending marriage of his daughter.

The Rendel Commission recommended a Legislative Assembly made up of thirty-two members, twenty-five of whom would be elected to four-year terms; and an Advisory Council of nine ministers to advise the governor. The ministers would be drawn from the political party that had the largest representation in the Legislative Assembly, in addition to British officials. The governor would have control over external affairs, defence and internal security. It wasn't complete independence, but a compromise between the colonial model and full autonomy.

This concept in part emerged due to Tan Chin Tuan's lobbying efforts for a slow transition to independence. Although he was proud of Singapore and the potential of its people to run their own affairs, he was all too aware that there were insufficient numbers of his countrymen capable of public administration.

The war had interrupted many students' education and the British had not helped foster the growth of tertiary education, which would have produced suitable candidates for government. Tan Chin Tuan had trouble filling positions in his own bank, much less the ranks of government. At the same time, he was fearful that full and immediate self-government might decimate the ranks of British civil servants in Singapore, creating a vacuum, much like that seen in Indonesia. Apart from the inefficiencies it would create, it could have led to a loss of stability. Indeed, there were already ominous signs.

In December 1950, the profound mishandling of a delicate racial issue had resulted in civil disorder. A little Dutch girl named Maria Hertogh had been raised by a Malay Muslim family after the Japanese in the Dutch East Indies interned her parents. After the war, a court in Singapore ruled that Maria had to be returned to her natural parents. Riots ensued. TCT discovered that the case had been badly mishandled by the police, in particular an inexperienced junior officer who had been too quickly promoted to a senior position. Lacking expertise, he had failed to contain the trouble before it spun completely out of control.

For Tan Chin Tuan, the Hertogh riot was a potential parable for Singapore — a not-ready-for-senior-office population left in charge of a newly independent country could cause havoc. There were other troubles as well during those years, suggesting political passions still ran ahead of reason, such as the May 1954 riots that festered out of a student demonstration in front of Government House. However, in the end, the British government agreed with the Rendel Commission's recommendations and scheduled elections for the new Legislative Assembly for April 1955. Singapore was to hold partial elections for the Legislative Assembly. (Full elections would be introduced four years later.) The appointed positions were to be replaced with elected ones, the number of seats was increased and the numerous political parties were preparing their campaigns.

The colony's leading political faction, the Progressive Party, led by the eminent Chinese politician, C.C. Tan, already had six of the nine elected seats in the Legislative Council. But the party relied on a small English-educated middle class electorate for support. With the heightened awareness of politics that emerged in the mid-1950s, the Progressive Party found itself out of touch with the broader electorate. It was facing keen competition from a variety of groups springing up on the left and right.

The party turned to Tan Chin Tuan in an effort to enlist his help. But TCT declined their invitation — he was exhausted and the prospect of campaigning did not appeal to him. Although there was clearly strong support for him running for office, he was averse to the rigours and indignities of the hustings. It struck him as unseemly. The essence of political campaigning is what TCT calls "crowing", boasting about one's accomplishments to the electorate and making promises that one might not be able to keep.

The Progressives repeated their pleas to TCT to campaign as an elected official. With him on their side they could defeat the Labour Front. But Tan Chin Tuan knew that it was time for his public life to come to a close.

In this turbulent climate and with such a prominent figure as TCT choosing to leave politics, the Progressive Party split in February 1955. A substantial portion of its members, who belonged to the Singapore Chinese Chamber of Commerce, broke away to form the Democratic Party, which sought to appeal to the Chinese electorate by advancing the cause of Chinese education and culture.

In the meantime, the public's attention turned to Lim Yew Hock, a well-known politician in the Legislative Council whom TCT had recommended for a seat. Tan Chin Tuan had helped Lim augment his meagre Legislative Council income by making him secretary of The Building Society of Malaya. Lim also split from the Progressives. He and a prominent lawyer named David Marshall formed the Labour Front out of remnants from the Labour Party, which had been founded in the late 1940s. Lim was a friend of trade unions but solidly anti-communist. Marshall was strongly anti-colonial. Under his guidance, the Labour Front stood for rapid transition to full independence and an end to the Emergency Regulations.

A year before the 1955 elections, a group of young British-educated Singapore residents, including Lee Kuan Yew, banded together to form yet another party dedicated to the end of colonialism and the building of an independent, non-communist Malaya and Singapore. They named it the People's Action Party (PAP).

On April 2, 1955, without TCT's presence in the election, the Progressive Party split the vote with the Democratic Party, enabling the Labour Front to win ten of the twenty-five available seats. Labour now had its mandate to seek a more rapid independence from Britain.

A new stage was beginning for Singapore and Malaya. But for Tan Chin Tuan it was the end of his public life and his remarkable role in the history of Singapore politics and government.

His decision to leave the political life was also influenced by an unpleasant new development. The long hours, onerous burdens and brutal pace he endured while simultaneously running the bank and the government were beginning to take their toll. One day in 1955, TCT began to experience a sudden, dull roaring in his ears. Rather than subside, it continued to worsen. Day after day he was tormented by the continuous sound. Doctors in Singapore could do nothing for him. He travelled to London to consult two Harley Street specialists, physicians so highly in demand that the only appointments he could get were in the evenings. They also could do nothing, other than identifying the intolerable problem as being linked to nerves.

Unwilling to give in, Tan Chin Tuan travelled to New York to see a ear specialist. From there, he sought another opinion from the Mayo Clinic in Rochester, Minnesota. After examining him, the doctor told TCT he was lucky — so far only his hearing had been affected. His ears had been the weak link in the chain and the first part of the body to buckle under the ruthless schedule he had been keeping. He was advised to slow down, or suffer dire consequences.

After the trip to Minnesota, TCT continued to consult other doctors, but they confirmed the diagnosis. The banker, whose life had been bursting with activity and accomplishment, found himself living in a progressively silent world and having to reduce both his workload and his commitments.

His achievements during the tumultuous ten years ending in 1955 had been remarkable. His service to the Rendel Commission was historic. As deputy president of the Legislative Council and based on his expertise in real estate, he was involved in the reconstruction and restoration of the Legislative Assembly building which was subsequently declared open by then Governor Sir John Nicoll on July 7, 1954. (After independence in 1965, the Legislative Assembly building was renamed Parliament House.) He had also served on a committee questioning freezing land values in advance of a master plan for Singapore. He had led many other vital committees, contained unrest on the labour front wherever he could and smoothed relations between the races. He had served on Singapore's first Board of Commissioners of Currency, determining the amount of funds to apportion to reserves.

Tan Chin Tuan reflected on the strenuous yet vigorous decade he had devoted in service to his nation. He had secured his place in the history books and built a network of influential friends, but at great cost to his health. As deputy president of the Legislative Council, he had overcome all racial barriers, achieving the highest position a British subject of Chinese descent could hold. Against this backdrop, he made the decision to concentrate his energy on the bank, his growing businesses and his corporate responsibilities. The results would be far beyond anyone's expectations.

Strikes, Turmoil and Independence

Tan Chin Tuan's public life may have ended, but his banking and corporate career was accelerating. Despite the burden of his duty to the Legislative and Executive Councils, the managing director of the Oversea-Chinese Banking Corporation had resolved by 1955 a myriad of immediate post-war challenges and initiated several progressive strategies to assure the smooth running of the institution.

Immediately after World War II, upon returning to Singapore, TCT's initial challenge was to re-establish the bank and restaff it with able, experienced employees. However, qualified men were in short supply as the war had decimated the bank's personnel. The Japanese had killed 12 per cent of OCBC's staff. Also, with little or no education in Chinese or English during the four years of Japanese Occupation, younger potential managers were without a solid education. Everything had to start anew.

In the early post-war years, TCT sent staff to Australia and England to upgrade their banking credentials. On their return, these young men helped train their colleagues. As he preferred his employees to remain in Singapore, TCT soon set up a training school and hired Wilfred Stanton, the former principal of the Midland Bank's training school, to run it. To encourage the British banker to work in Singapore, Stanton was furnished with an attractive house in Holland Hill, part of which was used for the classrooms.

The programme taught new skills to employees, as well as subjects that would advance their careers. The curriculum included typewriting, bookkeeping, shorthand and, naturally, banking and securities courses. The bank advanced the students money to pay the subsidised course fees, with the loan written off if they passed their examinations. TCT kept a watchful eye on his staff, encouraging and promoting those who excelled and moving the less talented to other positions to leverage on their individual aptitudes.

Staff welfare and morale were of prime concern. Even before World War II, as the founder and first president of the OCBC Staff Association, Tan Chin Tuan had nurtured his staff. The members paid a small fee and he persuaded the bank's chairman, Lee Kong Chian, to allocate some unused portion of the bank's premises to the staff association for its clubhouse. Its objectives were to foster esprit de corps, promote the advancement and improvement of members and improve their social, economic and general welfare. The bank organised picnics and other special events to demonstrate appreciation of the employees' diligence.

TCT expected three vital qualities in his staff — loyalty, talent and, particularly, integrity. Small mistakes were inevitable and were overlooked, but Tan Chin Tuan demanded complete honesty, without exception. But he also rewarded his staff, taking care of them as if they were family. One progressive measure was the OCBC Provident Fund, a type of pension fund modelled on a scheme initiated by the Shell group of companies. It proved so successful that the colonial government adopted the idea by legislating it in 1953 and putting it into force on July 1, 1955. Another generous OCBC programme awarded bonuses to its officers based on the bank's annual profits. Inspired by a similar strategy developed by Tan Kah Kee, this arrangement permitted the OCBC to pay salaries 3 to 5 per cent lower than rival banks, by offering large bonuses based on profit-sharing. At its peak, some delighted officers received as much as eight months additional salary on top of their annual wages.

The Oversea-Chinese Banking Corporation's board of directors was also delighted. TCT earned its unwavering support, due to the bank's sure and steady post-war growth under his stewardship. Most board members were substantial shareholders and their managing director had been reliably increasing their profits and capital. His strategy was simple and effective. After the war, some depositors felt safer entrusting their money to British banks than the locally incorporated ones. Tan Chin Tuan responded by charging his borrowers a lower interest rate, thus attracting business that the European banks had previously handled exclusively. There is a good reason for this strategy, as Tan explained in an interview with *Euromoney* in 1982: "Merely saying that the bank is solid as a rock does not make it solid. We strive to make it solid. For example, we pay a slightly lower rate of interest than most of our competitors on deposits with us and consequently are able to lend at a lower rate of interest to more selective borrowers and, hopefully, reduce our risk of bad debts." As the bank gained the trust and the deposits of the community, its status and reputation grew. The bank did not pay out more than 40 per cent of its profits in dividends. In that way, 60 per cent of the profits were applied to increasing the capital and strengthening the bank.

This is not to say that the stable growth enjoyed by the bank took place in an atmosphere of serenity. The twenty-one years during which TCT guided the bank as its managing director, from the end of World War II to his appointment as chairman in 1966, were turbulent for Singapore.

Historical changes were occurring, not only in Singapore, but also throughout all of Southeast Asia. The rise of militant politics exploded hand in hand with the growth of the trade union movement. Students, with little to lose materially, sought radical changes. Extremist political parties sought power. For some groups, violence or the threat of violence, was the only way their message could be heard. The communist-aided student riots in 1954 strengthened the Malayan Communist Party.

Activists were reviving the anti-colonial labour movement. The government ultimately responded by detaining subversives, including the MCP leaders. Agitators were expelled. Upheaval fostered uncertainty and stability seemed precarious. However, the purge benefited the non-communist members of the People's Action Party, particularly Lee Kuan Yew. The PAP came to power in the 1959 election, decisively winning forty-three seats.

The PAP government worked towards achieving industrial peace. Priority was given to the unification and strengthening of the trade union movement. The registrar of trade unions was empowered, through the Trade Unions (Amendment) Ordinance, to cancel the registration of splinter trade unions and avoid duplication in the workplace. By 1960, there was a power struggle between the moderate and leftist leaders within the PAP. This partition was also reflected within the labour movement. The Singapore Trades Union Congress was split into the leftist Singapore Association of Trade Unions (SATU) and the National Trades Union Congress (NTUC) led by the PAP moderates.

Although the NTUC took the same stance as the government on fundamental political issues, it was independent on trade union matters. Industrial issues such as wages and benefits led to frequent strikes and other actions. In a bid to foster better industrial relations, the government instituted the Industrial Arbitration Court in 1960 and passed the Employment Act in 1968. The 1968 Act provided the machinery for the regulation of relations between employers and employees, and for the prevention and settlement of trade disputes by collective bargaining, conciliation and arbitration.

The struggle between the NTUC and SATU continued. In 1962, the NTUC added several groups to its growing roster. The following year, the Registrar of Trade Unions refused the registration of SATU as a federation of unions on the grounds that it was used for unlawful purposes inconsistent with its rules and objects. By 1964, fifty-five registered employee unions, representing some 100,000 workers, were affiliated to NTUC. This represented 65 per cent of organised workers.

Throughout this climate of change, TCT kept a firm and steady hand on the bank and companies linked to him. But there were times when his patience was severely tested and negotiations with the unions began to resemble games of poker. It was difficult to know who was bluffing.

A potential strike at the Robinson department store was a case in point. The managers had caught two sales girls stealing and planned to sack them. Two rebellious unions were vying for the employees' support and each demanded that if the store didn't take the girls back it would strike. The managers had been unable to make headway with the union and turned to TCT for help. As chairman of Robinson & Company, Tan Chin Tuan's logic was simple, but effective. "If they strike, we'll close down the store. If the unions prevent us from firing staff caught stealing, the employees will continue to steal until there is no stock left. So we might as well shut our doors now."

TCT reiterated his intention to close the store in a meeting with one of the more radical union leaders. Admitting that common sense should prevail, the union withdrew its threat to strike. Now operating in an atmosphere of mutual respect, there was little trouble with the union afterwards.

Several years later, the same union chief was detained for being a communist. After serving a period in detention, he was permitted to leave for Britain to study law, on the proviso that he never return to Singapore. Tan Chin Tuan gave him some financial assistance and even provided an overcoat to keep the unionist warm in damp and rainy England. Although they had once clashed, TCT felt no animosity between them, considering the union leader not an enemy, but merely an adversary.

This example is one of the secrets of Tan Chin Tuan's success with people and one of the guiding principles of his life. He held no grudges. Never vindictive, he understood that people hold different points of view. He never allowed sincere and honest disagreement on issues to interfere with a cordial and courteous relationship with his opponents. The only people considered unworthy of respect were those who cheated or acted unethically.

Tan Chin Tuan resolved another labour problem, this time at OCBC, with cool-headedness and creativity. When mischievous unionists threatened to strike, worried depositors were concerned they would not be able to withdraw their money. In those days, even a rumour of trouble could panic customers and start a run on a bank.

TCT needed a way to reassure his customers that the bank was solvent. He ordered stacks of money to be visibly placed in a great block on a shelf behind the tellers. In addition, he made sure every counter was open by enlisting the bank's officers to substitute for the strikers. When the concerned customers arrived, they found very short queues — thanks to the excess of tellers — and a prominent wall of cash available. The effect was instant and reassuring. Their money was safe.

The dispute in question with the Singapore Bank Employees Union (SBEU) was over the status of some messengers employed by the bank. In July 1961, the union demanded its messengers be designated "clerical assistants", thus entitling them to a higher salary. TCT disagreed, as many of the couriers were illiterate and did not have the skills of the better paid clerical workers. This fact was proven by their inability to endorse their pay cheques as they couldn't even sign their names.

The union chose their moment to strike at a time when Tan Chin Tuan seemed vulnerable. He was in hospital, recovering from a gall bladder operation. His doctor was Dr Yeoh Ghim Seng, who had received his full surgical status thanks to TCT's intervention. TCT was informed that the bank employees were now on strike. TCT suspected that the SBEU had taken advantage of his hospital stay and misled the staff into striking. The union bosses failed to realise that even illness would not deter the resolute Tan Chin Tuan from his banking responsibilities.

TCT informed his surgeon that he wished to be discharged

immediately. "You are not yet healed, your stitches are still to be removed!" Dr Yeoh protested. But his impatient patient insisted.

Reluctantly, the doctor agreed to allow TCT to leave the hospital. Tan Chin Tuan quickly summoned the union leaders to his home. They were caught off guard and surprised to see him out of bed and ready to negotiate. With the managing director in hospital, they had calculated that OCBC would meekly agree to their demands.

TCT demanded that the unionists direct the striking employees to return to work. One leader tried to bargain for additional concessions, saying the workers would go back, provided that they receive remuneration for the time they were on strike. But TCT refused, arguing that if the employees hadn't worked they didn't deserve to be paid. "If you want them compensated, you pay them," he told the union leaders. "We cannot do so, as we have no money," one admitted.

The issue went to the Industrial Arbitration Court, chaired by Professor Charles Gamba. In his initial decision, Gamba ruled against OCBC, supporting the union's claim that the messengers performed clerical duties. The matter advanced to the Supreme Court, where Justice Ambrose reversed the decision and ruled that Gamba should try the case again. Although the atmosphere in the 1960s favoured unions, the bank eventually won the ruling. Years later, a retired Professor Gamba invited Tan Chin Tuan to lunch at the American Club. He wanted the banker to know that in the context of the times, he believed his initial decision was correct, but with the luxury of hindsight, he had changed his mind.

The strike affected all banks, as it prevented inter-bank clearing. This led to intervention by the PAP government, resulting in the passing of the Banking Bill in January 1962, under a Certificate of Urgency. The bill provided for a Government Clearing House to prevent further disruption to the banking industry during labour disputes.

With the strike over in March 1962, Tan Chin Tuan showed the forbearance that he had so often demonstrated in the past. Reflecting on the unionists' appeal for financial help for their members, he paid workers for their lost wages out of his own pocket. This generosity cost him $34,000, the equivalent of $300,000 today. When the bank's board of directors learned of this personal act, it offered to reimburse him. But TCT refused, deeply impressing the SBEU union leaders. One of them, the secretary, Wee Soo Chuan, came to see him. "I bow to you, Sir," he said.

During this time of labour unrest, the region suffered parallel political disruptions. In May 1961, Tunku Abdul Rahman, the prime minister of Malaya, proposed the creation of Malaysia. Singapore's prime minister, Lee Kuan Yew, supported the idea of merging and proposed a referendum. In August 1962, Lee announced that a common Malaysian citizenship would be granted to all Singapore citizens upon the merger. Six months later, he declared de facto independence for Singapore at the Malaysia Solidarity Day parade. On September 16, 1963, the Federation of Malaysia was proclaimed, embracing West Malaysia, Sabah, Sarawak and Singapore.

The honeymoon was brief. The following year, the People's Action Party put up token candidates for the March federal general elections in Malaysia. Its participation was seen as an attempt to challenge the United Malays National Organisation-led alliance. By July, the political tensions had become sharper and increasingly communal. The spiral slowly spun out of control as politicians exacerbated the situation with self-serving rhetoric. Riots broke out in Singapore during a parade to celebrate the prophet Mohammed's birthday.

The Malaysian Solidarity Convention was formed in May 1965 with the aim of achieving a non-communal, multiracial "Malaysian Malaysia." The concept raised the issue of immigrant rights and was seen as an attack on Malay special rights. Subsequently, at a UMNO general assembly, delegates called for the arrest of Lee Kuan Yew. In the end, Tunku Abdul Rahman was subjected to increasing pressure to have Singapore separated from Malaysia. The secession took place on August 9, 1965. Singapore was thrust into shaky independence.

Singaporeans worried if their country would have the fortitude and ability to succeed on its own. But Tan Chin Tuan held unwavering confidence in his country. He had watched Singapore evolve from an immature, colonial society, through the turbulent growth of nationalism, to a young but willing country, finally in charge of its own destiny. His dream of independence was a reality. It was time to sow the seeds of economic prosperity, play a pivotal role in the commerce of this island nation and see it thrive beyond its wildest dream.

Tan Chin Tuan demonstrated his commitment to an independent Singapore in practical ways. Regardless of which government was in power, he had always done his best to support his country, by helping with government loans.

Immediately after World War II, as Singapore developed rapidly, the colonial government had increasingly turned to local banks to finance its activities — a vindication of TCT's long-held belief that Singapore and Malaysia should rely less on British banks for the countries' finances. In 1949, as a member of the Legislative Council, TCT had supported a $4.3 million grant to Malaya, despite the fact that Singapore was still recovering from the ravages of war.

Seconding the motion for the grant, TCT said:

> "I think those who know me well will give me the credit of not being too free with money in my care. Nevertheless, let me declare forthwith that I support this motion whole-heartedly because I am convinced that it is not only desirable but also right and proper that Singapore should extend a sincere, helping hand to her neighbourly sister in her present financial plight... By making this sacrifice, we shall be able to console ourselves with the fact that we have done unto our neighbour what we would wish our neighbour to do unto us. We shall also have shown that our declarations of goodwill and sympathy to the Federation are not mere empty gestures but that we are prepared to back our words with deeds."

Four years later, TCT proposed the historic $30 million loan to Malaya, interest-free for ten years. The interest foregone represented a gift of more than $14 million.

The bank's support of government loans was not only patriotic, but also made good business sense. In 1958, when the municipal government floated a loan, TCT had suggested that the bank subscribe $1 million of the debentures. The government's own banks, the Hongkong and Shanghai Bank, and the Chartered Bank, however, had chosen not to participate in that particular debenture issue. Their decision angered the Singapore City Council and its mayor, Ong Eng Guan. The council declared that all monies held in the Hongkong and Chartered banks — tens of millions of dollars —should be transferred to OCBC, rewarding loyalty and participation.

Although grateful for this new and prestigious business, TCT was simultaneously concerned that the massive transfer would put extreme financial pressure on the Hongkong and Shanghai Bank. Telephoning the local manager, he inquired whether the bank needed a temporary infusion of funds to cover the massive transfer. TCT offered to quietly replace 75 per cent of the money the municipality was withdrawing, into the Hongkong Bank. In fact, the Hongkong Bank manager had planned to ask his head office to remit the funds to cover this substantial withdrawal. The next time TCT was in Hong Kong, the bank's chairman invited him to lunch. He expressed his appreciation of TCT's generosity and pledged to provide similar help should any OCBC branch in Hong Kong ever need it.

TCT not only participated in government loans but also assisted their syndication. When the first PAP government of 1959 approached TCT with its initial loan flotation (the issue of $15 million Singapore 5% Registered Stock 1959/67), TCT took on its placement. He began by committing OCBC to 25 per cent. Next he approached the Hongkong Bank, suggesting that, as the official bankers to the state government, it do the same. Naturally it agreed. He then went to the Chartered Bank, which confirmed that it would take its share, and finally approached the Mercantile Bank. Between these four senior banks, the loan was subscribed.

With independence, the PAP government required a vehicle to encourage new development within the island nation and formed the Development Bank of Singapore in 1968. The government approached TCT, who agreed to support the concept, and the issuance of 25 million shares of $1 each in the Development Bank of Singapore. He committed OCBC to $5 million and, in order to help the completion of the subscription, offered to take another $5 million if the DBS issue wasn't fully subscribed.

Later, when the Singapore government urged the locally incorporated banks to advance loans to Singapore Airlines to construct its new headquarters, TCT again helped arrange an orderly participation.

The loan, for 90 per cent of the building costs, was shared among all the institutions. The formula was based on total deposits, so that no one bank had to shoulder more than its fair share of the responsibility.

Throughout the turbulent decade of the 1960s, as he watched his nation endure the wrenching changes from colonialism to unification with Malaysia to outright independence, TCT continued to guide OCBC with a steady hand.

The social and political transformations had inspired Tan Chin Tuan to revise the bank's image. In 1962, TCT asked that the ancient Roman galleon that had long served as the symbol of the Oversea-Chinese Banking Corporation be replaced with a Chinese junk, to reflect its Asian heritage. Working with hand-picked marketing experts, TCT guided the redesign. He also sought a memorable slogan that would epitomise the qualities the bank was known for — reliability, stability and prudence. He wanted the phrase to correctly describe the bank as one that stood out from the riskier and more adventurous institutions more interested in business expansion than banking quality.

He had considered the motto "Save Safely and Sleep Soundly", and it certainly met his criteria. But TCT recalled a meeting with the Governor of Gibraltar, Admiral Sir Varyl C. Begg, and was reminded of the great imposing promontory at the entrance to the Mediterranean Sea, which stood as a symbol of strength and longevity. Thus the assuring slogan "Solid as a Rock" was born.

"Solid as a Rock" was the heart of a philosophy that had weathered the Depression, spanned the difficult war years and now fuelled the great expansion years. Tan Chin Tuan directed that the bank live up to its new motto and demonstrate its solidness. Cautious depositors must be assured that their money was safe. Buccaneers had no place in the Oversea-Chinese Banking Corporation. The bank sought stability, by both charging and paying lower interest rates. This in turn attracted the most stable customers.

Certainly, few men worked as long, hard and diligently as Tan Chin Tuan. And fewer had his remarkable stamina. As he is fond of saying: "Life is a marathon, not a sprint."

Even marathon runners need an occasional respite to reinvigorate them. TCT took his share of holidays but on one of them he survived a grim brush with fate.

In June 1964, he was invited by the Shaw brothers – Runme and Run Run – to the 11th Asian Film Festival in Taipei. Plans had been made to fly the party to Hualian and Taichung, on the other side of Taiwan. TCT and his wife initially declined to participate in those excursions. At Runme Shaw's urging, TCT subsequently agreed to go to Taichung but only if it was by car.

Eventually, the party, consisting of Runme Shaw and his wife Peggy, Tan Chin Tuan and his wife Helene, and friends Dr William Oh, Mr and Mrs Lim Koon Teck, Mrs Cecilia Kaan, Mrs Rosie Ho and Mrs Bebe Lim piled into several old cars and chugged uncomfortably along a bumpy road. By noon, the ladies were complaining. One of the vehicles suffered a punctured tyre. The inevitable delay and the stifling heat made the journey even more unpleasant.

Eventually, the party had to break journey and spend the night at Sun Moon Lake, a beautiful resort. While waiting for dinner, TCT, Dr Oh, Runme Shaw and Lim Koon Teck played mahjong. Suddenly, John Foo, one of Shaw's employees, ran into the room and gave them the horrible news that the C-46 aeroplane, on which they had been booked, had crashed, killing everyone on board.

Had Tan Chin Tuan, his wife and his friends taken the plane as originally scheduled, the crash would have taken their lives. But TCT had been adamant about not flying and the whole group had been spared.

Fate also intervened at the bank. OCBC's chairman Lee Kong Chian was diagnosed with cancer and resigned on January 28, 1966. After a courageous battle, he passed away the following year, aged 74.

The vice-chairman, Lee Choon Seng, briefly assumed the reins of power but he, too, had health problems and resigned within five months.

The bank's board of directors met and elected TCT to the chairmanship on June 24, 1966.

From its origins as a small bank, catering to one segment of the Chinese community, OCBC increased its shareholders' funds of $15 million in 1945, when TCT was managing director, to $70 million when he became chairman. During his tenure, these funds would grow further, to more than $1.1 billion. Over the next two decades, OCBC would become a solid, respected and powerful international bank. When TCT retired in 1983, OCBC's market capitalization would exceed $5.3 billion.

Acquisition and Growth

As the face of politics changed in Singapore, so did the central character of business. That evolution was to have an extraordinary impact on the direction and ultimate success of today's city-state. The growth of Singapore and its economy were exemplified, and in many ways led, by organisations like OCBC. Its holdings, both in the financial sector and in diversified other sectors, serve as a model of how Singapore transformed from a parochial and minor player in the British Imperial economy, into a modern one with a broader focus on Asia and the entire world.

The success of the Oversea-Chinese Banking Corporation had its genesis in the early years after World War II. Before the war, white colonials controlled almost all of the prestigious public companies. However, post-war politics throughout the region were perilous. The trading houses and financial outposts of the Imperial economy began to fade in tandem with the growing cries for independence. The communist revolution in China in 1949 and the Korean War between 1950 and 1953, created an uncertain environment for investors.

In Singapore, the inevitable progression toward self-government saw a corresponding reduction in the economic presence of the British. The emergence of radical politics and communist-led unions made British business leaders nervous. Strikes and work stoppages started in

1946 and increased as the labour movement gained power. Student protests escalated into riots by the mid-1950s. In this climate of political and social upheaval, with their political dominance clearly diminishing, the British lost the fortitude to face the uncertainty that came with independence. Instead, they opted to sell their shares and relinquish their companies, preferring retirement in rural England, or new ventures in business centres such as London.

Tan Chin Tuan strode into this vacuum. He recognised the British departure as an extraordinary opportunity to secure some viable businesses at attractive prices. Although the British were pulling out, demand for their companies' products and services remained. Singapore was growing rapidly and people had money to spend. As TCT reflected in a 1982 interview with the magazine, Euromoney:

> "There's a right time to buy and I was fortunate... to spot some good opportunities."

He also had confidence that the political instability would wane.

> "I was convinced that politicians who may appear radical in opposition, invariably become realistic and moderate when they are vested with responsibility."

Generally, the Chinese business leadership failed to share this sense of opportunity. British business practices were opaque and foreign, and not well understood by Asians. In addition, many Chinese businessmen did not speak English. They were unfamiliar with the British ways of doing business — of share holdings and trading, of the management techniques used, and the complex relationships between suppliers, customers and employees. Used to more clannish and inward looking operations, they had little experience in the European style of doing business.

As a banker, Tan Chin Tuan was aware of the concept of public companies and his political career gave him an ongoing relationship with the British, who regarded him as an ally. Hence, with little competition, TCT was poised to acquire participation in British-owned companies. His stature with the British made him the obvious choice of the European business elite. Thus it was natural that OCBC should be the first to be welcomed to participate in equity positions.

In one of those rare and fleeting moments in business history, Tan Chin Tuan was suddenly surrounded with bargains. Throughout the decade of the 1950s, the British were eager to sell off their holdings. There were so many companies on the market with so few buyers that the share prices of many sound and promising operations plummeted. Still, the bank avoided unrestrained investments, preferring to take a prudent partial interest in projects and companies run by people expert in their respective fields.

TCT applied strict criteria — the company had to be financially sound, had to have potential for growth and increased profitability, and the investment had to give him paramount authority in pivotal business decisions.

Under his leadership the bank gradually developed a network of blue chip corporations, leaving small-scale operations to other bankers and investors. TCT saw no reason, or profit, in snapping up every company in Singapore. His philosophy, at all times, is to look for intrinsic value and profit potential. He created mergers, as opposed to takeovers. He knew that takeovers, with their attendant hostility, could be more destructive than beneficial, creating resentment in the management ranks and confusion among the staff. Mergers, however, encouraged co-operation, working with co-owners, managers and staff, to expand the business prudently and for the benefit of all.

One of the bank's first forays into diversification stemmed, in part, from TCT's objection to racism and discrimination.

Before World War II, Raffles Hotel, a gleaming, white edifice with graceful, flowing palms, was a monument to European colonial society. It was the best place to see and be seen. The hotel register, bearing the signatures of the famous and influential, was testimony to the elite who enjoyed its hospitality: Somerset Maugham, Noel Coward, Charlie Chaplin, the great Belgian banker Baron Empain and archaeologist Peter von Stein Callenfels. Aristocracy, celebrities and the wealthy poured off the ocean liners, operated by P&O and Messageries Maritimes, to luxuriate in its ambience.

Raffles, along with the Adelphi, the Hotel de L'Europe and the Seaview, offered true Western luxury to diners and guests. The toast of Caucasian society in Singapore dined in its fine restaurant, the Tiffin Room, served by English-speaking Chinese "boys" (grown men, actually), wearing white jackets and trousers. The waiters, and some Indian clerical employees, were virtually the only Asians to be accepted inside the white portals of the hotel. Somehow, this distinction caused them to manifest the arrogance of their employers and treat members of their own race with indifference.

The rules were entrenched. Raffles was Singapore's finest hotel and it was to be enjoyed by the cream of society on the island, keeping in mind, of course, that the colour of cream is white.

In the 1920s, TCT had already experienced the sting of colonial racism at Raffles. He had to wait several hours for the Europeans to be served, before the waiters would take his order in one of the hotel's dining rooms.

The situation had not changed two decades later, when TCT, on behalf of OCBC, wanted to book rooms at Raffles for some business colleagues. He asked his assistant manager to telephone the hotel and make the arrangements. An abrupt receptionist informed the assistant manager that there wasn't a single room available. Every time, for the next few months, whenever OCBC staff members called, they were told that the hotel was completely full, which was not the case.

Chafed by such blatant discrimination, TCT called an old friend. Joseph Elias had also been a municipal commissioner and had enjoyed Tan Chin Tuan's hospitality in wartime India as a fellow member of the Malayan Association of India. TCT told Elias that he required hotel rooms for guests, but was being frustrated at the reservations desk. As a member of the board of directors of Raffles Hotel, Elias had influence. Within ten minutes, he phoned back. TCT's rooms had been booked for him.

This type of injustice happened all too frequently in colonial Singapore. It was a cause to be fought. Tan Chin Tuan was well known in his city as a diplomatic and courteous conciliator who could smooth over disagreements and persuade erstwhile combatants to work together. But he was also someone with courage, principles and conviction. Early in his business career he learned the necessity of defending one's self when under assault. He would never shy away from a battle in order to right a wrong.

TCT resented seeing others abused by people with power or influence. Time and again, often putting himself at risk, he helped those who did not have the strength or the ability to fight for themselves. He avoided electoral politics, preferring to serve his community quietly. And even after his formal political career had ended, he continued to fight bias behind the scenes, championing fairness and justice.

Tan Chin Tuan resolved that he would rectify the flagrant discrimination practised by Raffles Hotel. As the 1940s came to a close, he set his plan into motion. Steadily and efficiently, as they became available, he began acquiring shares in the venerable hotel on behalf of the bank. TCT's brother-in-law in Batavia worked in a biscuit factory. He heard that a block of 50,000 Raffles shares, owned by the family, was available and alerted TCT. When his friend Joe Elias died, his brother Isaac offered the entire 80,000-share block of Joe's holdings to Tan Chin Tuan. Quietly and methodically, he bought enough shares in the company, much to the surprise of the all-British board, to earn the right in July 1950 to sit as its first Asian director.

Five years later, Raffles' outgoing chairman, T. Aiken, retired to Britain. As the representative of the largest shareholder and with his corporate skills, TCT was the logical choice for chairman. However, some of the board baulked. The more subtle slyly suggested that he was too busy to take command of the hotel. Others, more overt in their hostility, submitted that his chairmanship might deter European business. "What do you know about hotels?" one director demanded. "I know nothing about hotels," TCT replied calmly, "But I shall employ people who do know how to run them."

The bank's substantial holdings in the hotel were persuasive and finally the reluctant European board members had to yield. TCT took control of the hotel with courtesy but firmness. One of his first tasks was to set aside a private dining room for OCBC's exclusive use. He also permanently reserved a suite to ensure that the bank's visiting guests could always have the choice of staying in Singapore's finest and most famous hotel.

Raffles Hotel had gone from being a humiliating reminder of Singapore's colonial past to become an emblem of equality and prestige. It was to serve the bank well. The venerable hotel became an effective public relations tool. It allowed TCT to entertain powerful and potentially helpful people with style and élan. Two such men were David Rockefeller, then president of the Chase Manhattan Bank, and George Champion, its chairman. In the late 1950s, on a reconnaissance visit to Singapore and finding Raffles fully booked, James Jacobson, one of the Chase executives, asked if it were possible for TCT to release a couple of rooms to the dignitaries. With his usual style, TCT arranged more than just a room. He orchestrated a VIP reception, complete with flowers and baskets of fruit in the hotel's finest suites.

Under most circumstances, it would have been difficult for TCT to secure a meeting with these important men. Yet, impressed by his hospitality, a day after the two Americans' arrival, Champion and Rockefeller asked to pay TCT a courtesy call to tender their appreciation of the luxurious surroundings. The two influential bankers became friends with Tan Chin Tuan, who saw to it that their visit was a pleasant one.

There was one unpleasant incident, however, which had an amusing outcome. George Champion complained of receiving an indifferent reception when he shopped at the Robinson department store. TCT phoned the store's general manager and discovered that the staff had been on the alert for an American confidence trickster who was supposed to be in town. They consequently viewed all Americans with suspicion! TCT requested that the Robinson general manager provide appropriate attention to its customers and when Mr Champion revisited the store, he was pleasantly surprised with the cordial reception.

The two New York bankers were so delighted with the lavish attention that they asked TCT if there was anything they could do to reciprocate. TCT demurred at first, but when they insisted, he gently suggested that raising OCBC's current credit line of $1 million at the Chase Manhattan might be helpful. The American bankers immediately offered an increase to $5 million, which TCT graciously accepted. His generous hospitality had paid dividends for the bank.

As the bank grew, the companies in which it had invested gained additional prestige. Synergy helped every company to grow, and that in turn helped the others. Most of the companies held a small position in one another, not enough to prove risky, but large enough combined to form a formidable block.

The bank headed this affiliation of business leaders in their respective industries. They included Great Eastern Life Assurance Company Ltd, Overseas Assurance Corporation, Fraser and Neave Ltd, Malayan Breweries Ltd, Robinson & Company Ltd, Wearne Brothers Ltd and Straits Trading Company Ltd.

TCT initially joined their boards as a director, eventually becoming their chairman. His success in guiding these companies is reflected in the annualised holding period returns (HPR) they gave to shareholders during his tenure. HPR is the total return on an annualised basis from holding an investment through a specific period, including dividends from the investment.

Using this investment performance indicator, Great Eastern Life led the pack with a 19 per cent per annum return during TCT's watch stretching thirty years. The other companies under his stewardship gave equally impressive returns. OCBC, in the financial sector like GEL, was a close second with an HPR of 18 per cent.

Malayan Breweries' HPR was 12.4 per cent while Fraser and Neave and Straits Trading Company had an HPR of 13.9 per cent each. Robinson's returns were 16.8 per cent and Wearne Brothers were 16.2 per cent.

Instead of being isolated profit centres, the interconnection between the companies under the TCT umbrella brought new efficiencies and strength to all. For example, it was suggested as each company joined the family, that it consider using OCBC as its banker but only if the bank's rates and services were equal to, or better than, the ones it was enjoying.

The bank was thus obliged to be nimble and competitive, but it was also assured of potential substantial business from the "group." Reciprocating, the companies helped to encourage business for the bank. Overseas Assurance encouraged its clients to borrow from OCBC. In turn, when mortgage borrowers came to OCBC, the bank referred them to Overseas Assurance for coverage.

Great Eastern Life Assurance Co Ltd, founded in the year of Tan Chin Tuan's birth, became the leading life insurer in the region. When TCT joined the board in 1962, insurance was still a new concept to many people in the region and premium and investment income totalled only $17 million. TCT became chairman of GEL in 1969 and profits grew substantially each year. By 1992, the year he retired from the company, income had soared to more than $1 billion, and it had a book value of $3.3 billion and a market value exceeding $4.3 billion. Considered a leader in innovation, Great Eastern Life was the first regional insurance company to computerise its operations. It also introduced creative new features, including its renowned Student Plan,

College Plan and Living Insurance products. Renewals, the litmus test of customer satisfaction, ran at 90 per cent in Singapore and 84 per cent in Malaysia, the highest of any insurer in Southeast Asia and among the best in the world.

Straits Trading Company Ltd was another success story. As one of the great British-founded companies in the region, Straits Trading Company, under TCT's twenty-seven-year chairmanship, saw its balance sheet increase fifteen-fold, all without a single rights issue to dilute per-share profits. Like so many other British companies after the war, ownership in the tin mining giant devolved from London-based holders to Malayan Chinese. By 1953, the stock was widely held by them and it was important that one of their own represent their interests on the board. In 1954, Straits Trading Company's chairman, Sir Ewen M.F. Fergusson, invited TCT to provide guidance as the first Asian on its board.

Straits Trading Company had become a ragged operation, with many unprofitable areas that required pruning. The Thailand Karak and Laboo mines were closed, followed by the shutting of the British Tin Smelting Co. subsidiary in 1961. New, more efficient operations, such as the sprawling Butterworth works, across the straits from Penang, opened in 1955. By 1965, Tan Chin Tuan had become chairman and Straits Trading Company had used its substantial reserves of liquid cash to diversify away from the volatile area of tin mining and smelting. It extended its investments throughout the region and as far away as Australia and New Zealand.

Occasionally, a British-dominated board of directors would challenge TCT's ascension to be chairman. The Raffles board had disputed his inexperience in the hotel industry. At Robinson & Company, the European directors questioned his lack of expertise in the retail sector. It was true that the lifelong banker knew very little about department stores. However, as in the case of the other businesses, he had the wisdom to rely on the assistance of competent people, who did understand retailing.

TCT carefully examined Robinson's accounts to determine what profit was being made and whether the return on investment was acceptable. He concluded that its returns were substandard and subsequently assessed the general manager's competence. Although the manager seemed to run the store well enough, TCT had no guidelines to gauge whether it could be managed more profitably. He commissioned an external assessment of the store. The report analysed the department store's operations and made a number of suggestions. It recommended moving the hardware department, with its low turnover and low margins, from the valuable main floor into the basement, freeing up the main floor for higher margin goods that could tap the higher traffic levels there. Robinson then rented the space previously occupied by hardware to an entrepreneur who sold ceramics, and returned three times the profit that hardware had yielded in the identical space.

Warming to the business of retailing, TCT asked his consultant to keep an eye on what goods were not selling. As buying patterns changed, Robinson could tighten its operations to yield a better profit. After a thorough study of how goods sold during a clearance sale, the consultant reported that larger apparel sizes weren't moving. Robinson had traditionally ordered clothes in all sizes. However, as the British had increasingly left Singapore, demand for larger sizes had diminished. Also, TCT learned that Robinson was in the habit of ordering all colours of clothing, even vile shades that no customer wanted. That practice was abruptly stopped. Slowly, making small adjustments here and there, retailing became leaner and more profitable at Robinson.

A number of the British sales staff had departed with the store's original owners. With his newly found understanding of retailing, TCT felt it was important to replace the sales people with employees who could speak Chinese. The new manager set about building up the ranks of sales staff who could speak their customers' language, thus bringing in more business.

The other department stores in Singapore failed to learn the lessons that TCT had discovered. Whiteaways, an established name in retailing throughout the British Orient, faded away because it continued to stock products catering to Europeans, even after the Europeans had left. John Little, the third British-founded department store, was initially taken over by the Hong Kong giant Jardine Matheson, but it too faltered and eventually Robinson bought John Little's assets. Just as Raffles was the only survivor of the three European hotels, so Robinson was the only European retailer to endure. Both had TCT as their chairman.

Disaster struck Robinson on the day of his 64th birthday. On November 21, 1972, Tan Chin Tuan was working in his office in Upper Pickering Street, when he noticed smoke coming out of the four-storey department store. A fire had started after an electrical short in the wiring in the basement. The flames spread quickly. Despite the valiant efforts of firefighters and Robinson's own employees, the blaze could not be contained and the store was reduced to rubble. Tragically, nine employees were killed in the blaze, some of whom were trapped in a lift when the fire took hold.

Robinson quickly found a new home in OCBC's new Specialists' Centre, Singapore's first high-rise multi-purpose complex. The Specialists' Centre on Orchard Road was itself a microcosm of the OCBC family, hosting branches of Great Eastern Life and OCBC itself, as well as the bank-owned Hotel Phoenix. Working night and day, the dedicated managers and staff of Robinson managed to set up and restock the department store at the Specialists' Centre. Within six weeks, a new store was operating in the new premises.

Another successful OCBC-linked company, Fraser and Neave, had originally been a printing company, which later expanded into soda water and soft drinks. Under British pro-prietorship, it had become renowned in the region for the quality of its beverages. From the time Tan Chin Tuan became chairman in 1957, until the company's centennial year in 1983, shareholders returns increased thirty-fold. Operations were added in Indonesia, Thailand, Brunei and throughout Malaysia.

During his twenty-five years as the chairman of Fraser and Neave, TCT visited the actual operation no more than eight times, so confident was he in the qualifications of the men he had put in charge.

After World War II, there were three aerated water brands sold in Singapore — Framrose, Phoenix, and Fraser and Neave. The first two disappeared, leaving F&N the sole domestic producer. F&N survived because the company's managers refused to raise prices. Instead, they expanded volume, moving aggressively to open branch operations in Malaysia and to transfer the bottling plant from Trafalgar Street to a larger tract of land in River Valley Road. The new plant created extra capacity and made Fraser and Neave a household name synonymous with beverages.

Besides its own brands of soft drinks, the company also bottled Coca-Cola, 7-Up and Sarsi under licence. Dairy products, Premier Milk and Meadow Gold ice cream, were manufactured under licence from the Carnation Company of the United States while Far Eastern brands such as Cow & Gate tinned milk were made from Australian and New Zealand powdered milk.

Malayan Breweries Ltd (MBL) was another drinks arm that proved to be a prudent investment. Founded in 1929 as a joint venture between Fraser and Neave and Heineken NV of Holland (the world's largest exporter of beer), Malayan Breweries was responsible for some of Southeast Asia's most popular brews, including Tiger Beer. At one point, Heineken was so enamoured with Malayan Breweries that it sought outright control. TCT thwarted the overture, foreseeing MBL's long-term prosperity in a thirsty climate. He blocked Heineken's advance by having a company which he headed buy up enough shares to give him the voting rights to stop the attempt.

Overseeing these diverse interests in the beverages market put TCT in a position to declare to visitors that they could not slake their thirst in Singapore without buying his products. "If you drink whisky, you must have soda. If you drink gin, you must have tonic. If you don't drink, you can have milk," he said.

As part of his strategy to link up synergistic companies, Tan Chin Tuan in 1979 convinced international can manufacturer Metal Box to sell a 35 per cent stake in its Singapore can factory to F&N and Malayan Breweries in return for exclusive-supplier rights. The two beverage companies had used the same approach when they bought a significant equity stake in a bottle manufacturer, Malayan Glass Factory Bhd, in Johore. In this way, both operations secured drink cans and bottles at reasonable prices, improving their competitive position and gaining additional profits from another reliable business.

The brewing business was profitable, but required business acumen and agility. When Malaysia and Singapore separated in 1965, TCT built a brewery in Malaysia to overcome both tariffs and Malaysian sensibilities about importing too many products. He also bought two breweries in Papua New Guinea, which reliably returned profits, until the Philippines brewing conglomerate San Miguel opened an operation there. The overproduction of beer affected the bottom line of both companies. TCT had earlier taken over the PNG operations of Australian Breweries and offered to do the same with San Miguel. Within three hours of talks, the company agreed to sell. The transaction allowed the San Miguel people a face-saving device, making it appear that they chose to sell to generate profit, not because their operation was losing money.

However, not every foray by Tan Chin Tuan into the brewing industry was about the nuts and bolts of plant and factory. Unprecedented growth and unbridled greed fuelled some entrepreneurs in the 1980s. They conducted business more like war and the first casualty was decorum.

Takeover fever infected the corporate world. Executives devoted as much energy to devising strategies to deflect corporate raiding, as they spent on managing their companies.

The stock markets of Australia and New Zealand in particular were characterised by frenzied buying and selling of shares of companies, often based no more than on rumours that they were to be taken over or were themselves about to mount a bid.

The corporate buccaneers sought to secure valuable entities, with a view to dissembling their structures and disintegrating their operations. By stripping the companies of their less productive assets, they sought to unlock value for themselves and their investors.

The key players on the prowl included such colourful personalities as John Elliott, Robert Holmes á Court, Bruce Judge, Alan Bond and, of course, Sir Ronald Brierley of Brierley Investments Ltd.

Brierley, from New Zealand, had built one of that country's largest conglomerates, mainly through contested takeovers. In 1977, one of his lieutenants, Bruce Judge, set his sights on Lion Breweries, a large NZ company in which Malayan Breweries held shares. Lion and Malayan Breweries also jointly owned Leopard Breweries, which was also based in New Zealand.

Judge went to Singapore to seek an interview with Malayan Breweries' chairman but TCT refused to see him. However, to protect the OCBC-linked companies' investment in the NZ breweries, TCT bought 18 per cent more of Lion.

The Lion board, in reaction to the various corporate developments, quickly developed a "poison pill" in the form of Androcles, a holding company designed to block any takeovers. (The name came from George Bernard Shaw's *Androcles and the Lion*, based on a Roman story of a slave thrown to the lions only to find that his feline opponent was one he had once helped by removing a thorn from the big cat's paw. The slave's supposed predator ended up being his grateful friend.)

Androcles Corp Ltd was set up with 50 million shares, half held by Lion and half by its chairman Sir Clifford Plimmer and director R.C. Bradshaw. Lion then issued 25 million shares (27 per cent of its own shares) to Androcles, in return for 25 million Androcles shares, ring-fencing Lion against a takeover. Shareholders endorsed the Androcles plan in a referendum. In the nervous environment of the prey, the Lion group did not understand that it was not in TCT's nature to make hostile bids. However, Brierley reacted by going to court to try and unravel the directors' scheme. The New Zealand press and stock exchange both condemned Androcles as manipulation for company control by a small managerial elite in violation of shareholders' rights, and the New Zealand Registrar of Companies refused to register the share exchange.

The following year, the New Zealand government passed legislation offering shareholders better protection from hostile raids. Lion shareholders voted for Androcles to cease holding Lion shares, thereby dismantling it as an anti-takeover instrument. The New Zealand business community learned that TCT had an aversion to corporate plunder. Even Sir Ronald Brierley, in his biography, publicly paid tribute to Tan Chin Tuan.

In late 1983, after TCT retired as chairman of OCBC, he and a few Singapore companies, some of which he headed, found themselves having to deal with another Antipodean takeover, this time in Australia. The events pitted TCT against one of that country's most powerful magnates, John Dorman Elliott, then the head of the Elders IXL Ltd (now known as Foster's Group).

The controversial takeover began with an attempt by Ronald Brierley to snatch a stake in Carlton & United Breweries, Australia's largest brewer with about half of the country's market, through a partial offer for 40 per cent of the company. This action triggered a counter-offer from Elders IXL because Elliott needed to defend his rear — CUB held 49.5 per cent of Elders, which in turn held some 4 per cent of CUB. With Brierley moving into a controlling shareholder position at CUB, it meant that Elliott's position at Elders would become vulnerable.

Elders' counter-offer of A$3.82 for the remainder of CUB it did not own, compared favourably with the Brierley partial offer at A$3.30. The tide turned quickly for Elliott and Elders, because Brierley made a fast exit, selling almost right away what he had accumulated in one week to the new on-market bidder.

Elders crossed the threshold of the 50 per cent plus one share condition of its offer and was well on the way to crossing the next threshold at 90 per cent, where it could compulsorily acquire the rest of CUB shares from any dissenting shareholder. All this before the formal offer document was even dispatched!

TCT, and other fellow Singapore CUB corporate investors, watched these developments with some consternation. For almost a year already, rumours had swirled around CUB about a possible tussle for control.

Firstly, CUB as a brewer was considered attractive by asset strippers. Its huge cash flow and undervalued properties, locked up in its countrywide network of outlets, was a potential gold mine. As a target company, its cash and property portfolio could be unlocked to finance its own takeover and still yield the predators a handsome profit.

Another reason for the rumours was that Elliott was uncomfortable with the cross-shareholdings that CUB and Elders had in each other. The market's view was that Elliott would have to act sooner or later to secure the Elders register before someone pre-empted him through attacking CUB. The CUB board was similarly uncomfortable with the prospect of having Elders swallow CUB. In early 1983, it began looking for strong long-term shareholders who would not sell at the first sign of profit.

TCT's reputation as a long-term shareholder was well known. It was also known that he liked brewers as investments because of their strong cash flow and large, under-valued property portfolios. Not surprisingly, he was identified as the stabilising factor that the CUB register needed.

In 1983, TCT, and some of the companies he led, were persuaded to take part in a placement of new CUB shares and subsequently, a one-for-five rights issue also. But less than a year after the Singapore investors went onto the CUB register, it looked as if they would be stampeded into selling at a profit, but not at what they believed to be the intrinsic value of their CUB investment.

Their uneasiness was not lessened by their belief that the Elders offer substantially undervalued CUB. This view was confirmed when an independent valuation, by Australian broker Potter Partners, required under takeover laws to enable directors to advise minority shareholders, showed that the shares could be worth as much as A\$4.80 each.

To protect their interest, Singapore shareholders of CUB, including TCT, raised their holdings gradually and in a disciplined way. They paid only a few cents above the Elders offer price. When Straits Trading Company neared the 5 per cent level, it declared the size of its holding to CUB.

The rest of the Singapore shareholders held much less, but as TCT made clear to John Elliott when the two men met, he could only advise the other Singapore investors, not compel or coerce them to accept or reject the Elders offer. Indeed, Malayan Breweries (now known as Asia Pacific Breweries), of which TCT was the chairman, did accept the original Elders cash offer.

The attempts to pressure TCT into selling escalated, concluding with Elliott himself arriving in Singapore. Over lunch, Elliott made his threat. With 80 per cent control of the company, he might refuse to pay out dividends. Tan Chin Tuan was unfazed. Why would the minority share-holders mind, he inquired calmly, if the 80 per cent shareholder forgoes his dividends also? Elliott could not afford the luxury of being unflustered. His empire was built on debt. He needed that dividend income but more pertinently, Elders needed to have full access to CUB's cash flow and assets, to finance the A\$1 billion debt it had taken on to buy up the brewer.

Threats aside, Elliott also offered alternatives, other than an on-market higher buy-out price, to compensate the Singapore investors, but because these were not transparent, they were rejected. The square-off prompted a Melbourne newspaper, *The Age*, to play on OCBC's Solid as a Rock slogan: "Elders IXL must now be getting the nasty feeling that it has run into an immovable object." Finally, a frustrated Elliott was obliged to offer A$4.56 for the Singapore investors' shares (74 cents above his original offer price). That profit was worth S$70 million at the then prevailing exchange rates.

The frenzied quest for growth at any cost came to an abrupt halt in October 1987 with the resounding crash of global stock markets. Fortunes were lost, highly leveraged entrepreneurial groups simply vanished and the world financial markets were rudely shocked back into reality.

Events around the world in subsequent years fuelled the volatile financial situation. The Gulf War suspended meaningful commerce in the region and heightened fears of an oil crisis. The breakup of the Soviet Union and the shattering of the Berlin Wall, led to profound political uncertainties. In China, the Tiananmen Square crisis drew attention to difficulties within the country's leadership.

Few business leaders survived these turbulent times with their reputations intact. The winds of change blew harshly on many, but kindly on Tan Chin Tuan. His international reputation for fairness and integrity was sealed during this decade of chaos. Even after his retirement from the bank in 1983, the former OCBC chairman continued to be praised for his loyalty to shareholders, fidelity with depositors and honour within the marketplace. The "Solid as a Rock" slogan was as appropriate to TCT's status as it was describing the intrinsic strength of the companies under his leadership.

International businessmen who admired his perspective, sought his advice. Few leaders had his experience, he having witnessed the vagaries of several business cycles dating back to the early years of the century, through the political changes within Singapore, to the frenzied global markets of the 1980s.

Tan Chin Tuan would suggest that risky investments be rejected, as "it is better to miss out on a profit than to incur the loss of capital." He would caution the listener to "never swim against the tide of the markets", reasoning that a swimmer who went against the flow might succeed in reaching his objective, but was more likely to be weakened by his efforts, even to the point of drowning before the tidal direction changed. Instead, the swimmer would be advised to maintain his relative position within the tidal flow to conserve strength, so that he might have the energy to not only go with the flow, but forge ahead of it when the market turned. Many of the executives who heeded this advice prospered.

Tan Chin Tuan warned against over-leveraging the balance sheet for the purpose of commercial growth through acquisition. He reminded them of the effects of the crash of the rubber markets during the 1920s and stock markets during the 1930s, leading to a depression that wiped out many good men and good companies, because they did not have the cash reserves to survive the downturns. It was the avowed philosophy of TCT to ensure that companies under his chairmanship build sufficient cash reserves to survive two or three years' depression.

TCT was willing to invest his own resources and lead the investment of the resources of companies within his scope, in a manner consistent with these conservative principles. The annual returns on investments under his influence, from the end of World War II through to the close of the 1980s, exceeded a compound annual rate of 13 per cent — a performance rate equalling those achieved by legendary value-oriented international fund managers.

During his career, TCT served 287 years as a director of the various OCBC-linked companies and 171 years as chairman of nine public companies. His longest tenure was with Overseas Assurance Corporation, lasting more than forty-four years. With TCT at the helm, shares in the bank and the companies under its umbrella, had become a bellwether for the Singapore bourse, their movements often signalling the direction of the overall market.

These companies became synonymous with stability, reliability and investor loyalty. Shareholders enjoyed the double benefits of regular dividends as well as unparalleled stability and consistency.

And throughout TCT's tenure, none in the OCBC stable, with the exception of the bank, ever made a rights issues. Under the chairman's careful nurturing, there were always enough retained profits, after paying dividends, to finance expansion or undertake diversification.

Consequently, shareholders came to enjoy regular bonus-issue shares given to shareholders "free", which were financed by capitalising retained profits to enlarge the issued capital base. For example, an investor who bought 1,000 shares in Great Eastern Life when TCT became a director and held them until his retirement as chairman, would have seen those shares grow to 16,700, all this without having to fork out a single extra cent after the initial investment.

OCBC made rights issues for three reasons: Banking regulations had tied the amount of business a bank could do and the deposits it could take to the size of its capital base; Singapore's economy grew rapidly during the 1970s and 1980s; and the stiff foreign competition that was allowed in the banking sector even then. OCBC's capital base was also enlarged through shares it issued to merge with Four Seas Bank and a strategic stake in Hong Kong's Wing On Life.

However, TCT did not allow the bank to exact the maximum premium that it could for its rights issues. Instead, rights issues during his tenure were priced at substantial discounts to the market price — as low as $3 — mainly to be accessible to small shareholders. For investors who could not afford to take up their rights despite the steep discount, they could sell their entitlements in the market for an attractive windfall.

Hence, OCBC's rights issues, unlike most rights issues made by other companies, invariably led to a rise in the price of the mother shares, as they were perceived to contain a substantial bonus element.

Tan Chin Tuan once told a shareholder meeting, "The secret of survival and continuing prosperity is by a cautious and sound course." TCT set that sound course and the bank avoided speculation in favour of growing businesses of genuine quality, long-term profitability and service to the public.

Although his critics suggested that TCT could have expanded (and risked) the OCBC business more, the banker was never willing to compromise the bank's core value, "Solid as a Rock". His strategy was to return strong profits both consistently and honourably.

Innovation and Diversification

One of Tan Chin Tuan's enduring characteristics is his ability to inspire friendship and loyalty. His charm and thoughtfulness attracted friends and admirers of all nationalities and political stripes. The colonial government saw him as pro-British. China believed he was pro-Chinese. Malaysia considered him a friend, and Singapore of course counted him as an intensely loyal pioneer.

The reality was that TCT was simply his own man. Yet he had an intense understanding of human nature and could appreciate all points of view. Governments and corporations sought his advice and he was in great demand, receiving more offers to sit on corporate boards and government committees than he could accept. But he was generous with his time and took on commitments for projects he deemed important.

His association with the Malaysian government, as a member of the Board of Commissioners of Currency, and with numerous corporate ventures that benefited the Malaysian economy, led that government to confer on him the honour of Panglima Setia Mahkota, which permits the recipient to bear the title "Tan Sri".

As this was an external honour, he requested and received the approval of the Singapore government before accepting the distinction. Thus in a solemn ceremony in 1969, His Majesty, the Yang Di-Pertuan

Agong of Malaysia, presented the prestigious order, which entitled him to be known as Tan Sri Tan Chin Tuan.

Not one to rest on his laurels, Tan Sri Tan continued to dedicate himself to his extensive banking and corporate commitments. He was by now chairman of some of Singapore's most important companies — Great Eastern Life, Overseas Assurance Corporation, Fraser and Neave, Malayan Breweries, Raffles Hotel, Robinson & Company and Straits Trading Company. He skillfully balanced these responsibilities without adversely affecting his primary duty as chairman of the Oversea-Chinese Banking Corporation.

Tan Chin Tuan's secret was a superb work ethic and an ability to be fully prepared, as reflected in the comparatively brief board meetings he would conduct. Meetings rarely lasted more than ninety minutes, half what most other chairmen might take. TCT prepared rigorously for all meetings. It was not unusual to see him leave the office at the end of a long day with four or five briefcases in tow. During board meetings, he would crystallise his arguments into a single point that could be grasped quickly and completely. He always sought and considered the views of the other directors so that the relevant board could reach its decisions harmoniously.

Guided by Tan Chin Tuan, the Oversea-Chinese Banking Corporation expanded during the post-war years into areas that would have astonished its founders. In 1969, OCBC applied for a licence to open a branch in the United Kingdom. The branch enabled OCBC to increase its role in the Asian dollar and gold markets, and handle its customers' pound sterling investments. Bank of England officials in charge of granting banking licences initially placed restrictions on the banking activities OCBC could undertake, but when TCT politely but firmly suggested that he would appeal to the Governor of the Bank of England, the officers agreed to remove any restrictions.

On August 4, 1969, Tan Chin Tuan gathered with some old friends and associates in Cannon Street for the inauguration of the London branch. Those attending included Sir Franklin Gimson, the retired Governor of Singapore, and Sir Ewen Fergusson, TCT's predecessor at Straits Trading Company. The business relationships forged throughout his years as managing director and as chairman, extended the bank's constellation of friends worldwide — from David Rockefeller of the Chase Manhattan Bank, to Harry Oppenheimer, the patriarch of Anglo American Corp, the giant South African conglomerate.

Between 1970 and 1973, Singapore experienced a mini-boom and the bank began to expand internationally. TCT led the bank into innovative new initiatives that complemented its traditional banking. These included several joint ventures with foreign banks, which helped OCBC to spread its wings and become a truly global player, while simultaneously limiting the risk.

One of OCBC's first joint ventures was First Oversea Credit Limited (FOCL), incorporated in 1970 together with First National City Bank of New York. FOCL specialised in industrial financing, particularly equipment leasing, and quickly established itself as one of the leading industrial financiers in Singapore. In 1977, OCBC's American partner decided to sell off minority stakes in overseas companies and consequently sold its 14 per cent share in FOCL to Britain's Midland Bank. The company was renamed Forward Overseas Credit Limited, to retain the FOCL acronym.

OCBC and the Midland Bank had enjoyed an association that stretched over several decades. TCT initially received a somewhat cool reception on his first visit to London. At the time, OCBC was merely a $10 million bank and thus only worthy, in the British bank's eyes, to meet with the manager. Later, he was received by the assistant general manager. It was not until the chief general manager of the Midland Bank visited Singapore in the early 1950s that the association blossomed. W.G. Edington had lost a leg during the war and walked with some difficulty, using crutches. As deputy president of the Legislative Council, Tan Chin Tuan was permitted to drive his limousine onto the airport tarmac to personally greet and drive Edington out of the airport. This thoughtfulness was appreciated and the goodwill and relations between the two banks fostered and strengthened.

Singapore International Merchant Bankers Ltd (SIMBL) was another international joint venture, this time linking OCBC with Continental Illinois National Bank and the Crown Agents and Alexanders Discount Company, both of Britain. SIMBL, also established in 1970, became a major merchant bank in the Far East, providing advice to important companies that were reorganising or merging. However, the 1973 to 1974 oil crisis adversely affected the merchant bank in its early years and TCT decided it needed more capital.

As OCBC owned 50 per cent of SIMBL, Tan Chin Tuan spearheaded the fund-raising effort. En route to the World Bank meeting in Washington, TCT stopped over in Chicago to see his Continental Illinois counterparts, who had a 20 per cent stake in SIMBL. A vice-president of the Continental Illinois initially indicated to TCT that the American bank was not keen to put in more capital.

Tan Chin Tuan had spent a lifetime resolving difficult situations. During lunch, he and the bank's president discussed his plan. By the time coffee was served, Continental Illinois' president had agreed to inject more funds into SIMBL.

Accompanied by Dr Tony Tan, Tan Chin Tuan then flew to London. Although he was pre-warned that the Crown Agents would likely decline his call for fresh capital, he still sought and secured a meeting. Ushered into a large boardroom with a long narrow table, TCT and his associates sat on one side. The Crown Agents' officers took their seats on the opposite side. A large door at the other end of the room suddenly opened and the head of Crown Agents joined the discussions. After listening carefully to TCT's submissions, the chief agreed to join in the rehabilitation of SIMBL.

TCT's globetrotting intervention was successful. With a fresh capital infusion, SIMBL strengthened and became a leading merchant bank in the region.

OCBC's presence was also felt in Japan. In 1972, OCBC had opened a branch in Tokyo to serve as an operations base for Asian dollar, gold market and foreign exchange dealings, as well as a conduit for information about Singapore and Malaysia for Japanese clients of the bank. The same year, the bank formed a partnership with Yamaichi Securities, one of Japan's largest securities traders, in yet another international joint venture. The Singapore-Japan Merchant Bank specialised in financing Japanese joint ventures in Southeast Asia and participating in the Asian dollar bond market. SIMBL and the Bank of Tokyo were also involved. The initiative was special in that it balanced lending with underwriting, in contrast to other Singapore-based merchant banks, which relied on underwriting alone.

During his later years of service to the bank, TCT presided over many innovations that went against the bank's reputation as conservative.

One undertaking was the International Bank of Singapore (IBS), a consortium bank formed in 1973 by OCBC, the Development Bank of Singapore, United Overseas Bank and Overseas Union Bank. Each took a quarter share in IBS, designed as a vehicle to establish Singapore's banking presence internationally and enable shareholder banks to participate in overseas expansion. TCT served as its first chairman and his alternate director was Dr Tony Tan.

Just as the three small Chinese banks had come together in 1932 to form OCBC to optimise their strength, the consortium bank similarly leveraged on their shareholders' combined resources, enabling IBS to set up in territories that limited the number of foreign banking licences issued. Branches were established in Taiwan, Korea, the Philippines, and the United States. Unfortunately, less than a decade after IBS was formed, its performance fell short of initial expectations. In the end, it was decided that IBS should be bought out by one of the four share-holders via tender. OUB offered the highest bid, and IBS became its wholly-owned subsidiary.

In 1973 too, OCBC merged with the smaller Four Seas Communication Bank, allowing both banks to enjoy a greater base upon which to provide specialised banking services to large-scale industries with their increased financial and technical needs. The enlarged OCBC was also better placed to serve a wider range of customers and its products were as extensive as they were profitable.

Another innovation undertaken during the breakneck pace of the 1970s had far-reaching consequences — the carefully considered move by OCBC into computerisation. Today computers are commonplace at work and at home, and used for business and recreation. As a universal part of everyday life, they are consequently taken for granted.

But in the 1970s, when OCBC made the vital and progressive decision to computerise, the electronic brain's impact was less clearly understood. Computers at that time were mostly restricted to very large data-gathering companies, utilities and major international corporations. Little was known about them outside these areas.

Tan Chin Tuan counselled a cautious appraisal of the new technology, preferring not to rush blindly into something until it had proved more than a passing fad. First there was the issue of confidentiality — paramount in any financial institution's business relationship with its customers — and TCT demanded that such concerns be addressed.

By 1976 the bank was fully computerised, becoming the first local bank to provide online service to all its savings, fixed deposit and current accounts. Implementation was systematic and scrupulously organised. Technological efficacy was assured. Adhering to TCT's instructions, at no time were day-to-day operations seriously disrupted by the computer's arrival. Nor was confidentiality ever breached.

During the time that computerisation was being introduced, a landmark event in TCT's career took place — the celebration of his fifty years with the Oversea-Chinese Banking Corporation and its predecessor, the Chinese Commercial Bank. An evening of festivities was held in the Island Ballroom of the Shangri-La Hotel on March 1, 1975. One thousand employees, bank officers and distinguished guests honoured a half-century of selfless service to banking in Singapore.

The evening began with an emotional standing ovation and resounding applause for the popular banker. Speeches paid tribute to TCT's contributions to the bank and the nation. On behalf of the directors and management, Yong Pung How spoke as follows:

> "On March 1st, 1925, Tan Sri Tan Chin Tuan joined the old Chinese Commercial Bank as a clerk and thereupon commenced his unique record of outstanding service with the OCBC Group. Tonight we honour him for the first 50 years of this service. Fifty years is a long time, and for this reason alone it is unlikely that our fast changing times will let his record of service be repeated in local business history.

> "But tonight we also honour Tan Sri Tan as an outstanding leader of the business community, whose ideas and actions for the greater part of these 50 years have had the most significant and lasting impact on the economic life of Singapore and Malaysia, who, as far as it is possible for a man to be, has come to be regarded as a financial institution, personifying the hard work, determination, common sense and scrupulous adherence to principles, which are the hallmarks of the true banker."

The highlight of the evening was a presentation to Reginald Quahe, the deputy vice-chancellor of the University of Singapore (now the National University of Singapore). In commemoration of his half century of service to Singapore's banking and business community, OCBC created the Tan Chin Tuan Professorship in Banking and Finance at the National University of Singapore.

When TCT rose to the podium, an emotional crowd again thundered its applause. Addressing the gathering, TCT modestly credited the bank's prominent position to "the collective efforts of its dedicated and devoted directors and employees, past and present".

But those attending that glittering evening knew that Tan Chin Tuan's contribution was beyond calculation. He had guided the bank tirelessly, co-ordinating its activities to take advantage of post-war prosperity and nurturing a reputation that was without equal anywhere in world banking. Without his steadfast direction, the bank might never have achieved its pre-eminence.

Tan Chin Tuan is not a man to dwell on the past. But in a rare moment of reminiscing publicly, he noted in his speech how Singapore and OCBC had changed. "Today we pay to see tigers in a zoo," he said, recalling his early days on the rubber plantations when his party once encountered a real tiger, with nothing more to defend themselves but an umbrella. "Sad to say," he chuckled, implying that the world of finance was akin to a jungle, "such a hair-raising experience could evoke little response from me now."

"The banking world in those early days was dominated by foreign banks who under the shade of the colonial umbrella monopolised all foreign exchange dealings and the custom of the large trading houses, which were almost all British. Like the other Chinese banks in Singapore, our bank had to be content with the crumbs, and our business was mainly with the small Chinese firms and individuals. One of the greatest satisfactions to me is that over the last three decades, OCBC has managed to develop into the leading bank in Singapore with branches in a number of capital cities, and a complete network of international ramifications... I consider myself most fortunate to have witnessed from within, the birth of OCBC in 1932, and its growth and progressive development ever since."

TCT gave generous credit to the men who had been his mentors at the bank and in the community: Dato Dr Lee Kong Chian, Chee Swee Cheng, Tun Sir Tan Cheng Lock, Dr Lim Boon Keng, Lee Choon Guan, Tan Ean Kiam, Lee Choon Seng, and, of course, Tan Kah Kee.

Among the many honours that Tan Chin Tuan received on his 50th anniversary of service was a message, in the form of a Chinese scroll. It was a gift from the man, whom along with Tan Kah Kee, TCT most admired, Dr Chang Kia Ngau, the former General Manager of the Bank of China. The metre-long scroll remains one of TCT's most treasured possessions. Decorated ornately in red and gold, the inscription reads as follows:

SOLID AS A ROCK

A tribute by Kia-ngau Chang
to his lifelong, esteemed friend
Tan Chin Tuan, on the 50th
anniversary of his banking service.

"From 1910 to 1919 three banks were successively established in Singapore the Chinese Commercial Bank, the Ho Hong Bank and the Oversea-Chinese Bank. In 1932 these banks merged to form the present day Oversea-Chinese Banking Corporation. From modest beginnings, this bank has successfully grown, developed and matured over a remarkable 42-year lifetime.

"From 1945, Mr Tan Chin Tuan has been in charge of the operations of the entire bank. Under his direction, the bank has made great strides forward. Its reputation has been greatly enhanced. Increased public confidence has supported the bank's growth into the foremost financial institution in the state of Singapore. In international banking, it now operates on par with the leading financial institutions of the world.

"Mr Tan Chin Tuan joined the Chinese Commercial Bank in 1925, seven years before the merger of the three banks. After the merger, he continued in the bank and undertook several important positions. At the beginning of World War II he travelled to China, Burma, India and Australia to find an appropriate place outside of occupied Singapore in which to preserve the assets of the bank. After the end of the war, he made great efforts to re-establish the bank and infuse it with a sense of new goals and direction.

"The present stature of the Oversea-Chinese Banking Corporation and the solid foundation on which it stands represent the crystal of Mr Tan Chin Tuan's lifetime of devoted and untiring efforts.

"I am sending four words from an ancient Chinese proverb... meaning solid as a rock, to commemorate Mr Tan Chin Tuan's brilliant accomplishments in his 50 years of service in the bank."

— March 1, 1975

Dr Chang was a man whom TCT revered, and the OCBC and the Bank of China had a long history of mutual benefit, thanks to the two men's cordial relationship. TCT never forgot Chang's faith in OCBC's predecessor bank, when he had injected an investment to help the CCB during its currency exchange crisis. Later, as China's Minister of Communications, Dr Chang had also arranged for Chinese post offices to act as the Chinese Commercial Bank's agents. By distributing small remittances from the overseas Chinese to relatives back home, it enabled CCB to reap a profitable share of the remittance market in Singapore.

Even after Dr Chang left the Bank of China, TCT continued to stand by that institution. In the early 1960s, the Malaysian government (which had power over Singapore at the time) decided that no foreign government-controlled banks could operate in its territory, particularly not a communist-owned bank. Consequently, it ordered the closure of all Bank of China branches in Malaysia and Singapore. The Singapore branch manager of the Bank of China feared that this action would result in a run by its depositors. He asked Peking (now Beijing) to transfer funds from the bank's London offices to meet any withdrawals, but Peking refused.

Tan Chin Tuan was concerned. He knew that a run on one bank could ignite panic runs on other banks. He quickly met with the Bank of China's Singapore branch manager. He offered to make funds available to cover any excessive withdrawals. He would hold the deeds to two Bank of China properties as collateral. The Malaysian Central Bank denounced the move, accusing TCT of aiding a communist organisation.

Malaysia's Finance Minister, Tan Siew Sin (the son of Tan Cheng Lock, one of the directors of OCBC, who spent the war in Bangalore), and Prime Minister Tunku Abdul Rahman recognised Tan Chin Tuan's move was altruistic as well as practical, and was not an endorsement of communism. Mindful of the sound financial advice TCT had given their government over the years, they supported his actions. Tan Chin Tuan's lifelong friendships and reputation for fairness helped him avoid any troublesome consequences. However, criticism from the Malaysian officials would not have deterred him from helping. TCT was not one to turn his back on an old friend or benefactor. And on that night of nights, on his 50th anniversary, his friend Dr Chang remembered and honoured him for this quality.

Much had occurred during that half century. OCBC had spread its influence far beyond Singapore's compact boundaries. Under Tan Chin Tuan's leadership, the group's powerful voice was now heard throughout the region and around the world. By the mid-1970s, the OCBC had achieved international prominence. It was now a respected institution of unimpeachable quality and integrity, thanks to its long serving chairman.

Yet, even as he passed his 50th year of service, there was more to be done. There was one more major project in the works — a landmark, which would become a tangible and lasting monument to the career of the banker, Tan Sri Tan Chin Tuan.

The Changing Skyline

OCBC had grown into an international bank rivalling its foreign competitors for influence in Southeast Asia. Tan Chin Tuan saw the bank needed new headquarters to reflect its stature and image.

The China Building had served OCBC well for close to four decades. Tan Chin Tuan had a personal affection for this structure, having overseen its construction in 1932. Major Keys, who also created Singapore's stately general post office, the Fullerton Building, designed the six-storey bank which was an imposing edifice in a street of low-rise shophouses. Built in traditional Chinese architectural style, the China Building had a dramatic green-tiled slouching roof, and was adorned with ornate white pilasters upon which "Oversea-Chinese Banking Corporation" was inscribed in Chinese characters.

The building was recognised as a Singapore landmark and had even graced the nation's postage stamps. But by 1970, the grand old lady of Chulia Street was no longer big enough for the bank's growing activities. OCBC had outgrown the confines of its venerable home. It was time to create a new home to reflect the bank's growing stature and future prominence.

The new bank building had to be a concrete manifestation of the bank itself. Symbolically it was important that it should appear as contemporary as the modern services it provided.

Tan Chin Tuan visualised a building that would physically reflect the bank's core values of lasting strength, continuous growth and uprightness. But wishing to conserve its reputation as a conservative and trustworthy financial institution, expansion without disruption required bold, yet prudent steps.

A structure of this significance required the best. It was fitting that one of the world's foremost modernist architects would be approached to work with one of the banking industry's foremost architects. Ieoh Ming Pei, born in Canton and based in the United States, had been responsible for some of the most important buildings of the post-war period. His creations included the East Building of the National Gallery of Arts in Washington, D.C.; the master plan for Columbia University in New York; the fifty-four-storey headquarters for the Canadian Imperial Bank of Commerce in Toronto; and the seventy-storey triangulated Bank of China building in Hong Kong. His reputation as one of the twentieth century's premier architects was already established when he designed his career's crowning glory, the astonishing and exquisite glass pyramid entrance to the Louvre in Paris.

TCT held several informal discussions with Pei, and in May 1969, TCT met with the architect, intending to formally commission him to design the new headquarters.

Initially, Pei declined, pleading overwork. In fact, he was en route to a well-earned vacation and visit with his father, Pei Cho Ee, a friend of TCT's. However, when the architect told his father about the potential assignment, the elder Pei commented that it would give him personal pleasure if his son would design this important project for TCT. The following day, I.M. Pei telephoned the OCBC chairman and accepted the commission.

Tan Chin Tuan's vision was of a building that would reflect the bank's slogan "Solid as a Rock". A common story circulated that in an early meeting with his new architect, TCT tried to convey his dual goal of strength and stability. Dramatically, he lifted his arms and formed two fists. Pei, who is fond of drawing, sketched TCT's arms on the back on an envelope. This gesture may have been the original inspiration for the twin cores that became the backbone of Pei's design. The architect prepared many models before presenting his final submission for approval.

While Pei concentrated on the design, TCT considered the funding. He vowed that the entire $100 million cost of construction should be derived from shareholder capital rather than debt. A rights issue, of one new share of $10 for every $100 stock held, was fully subscribed. Financial prudence, even in erecting a valuable economic asset, such as the new building, was still the policy at OCBC.

For more than a decade, Tan Chin Tuan had been accumulating the requisite land by carefully acquiring the buildings around the China Building as they became available. To complete the parcel, he also required and received the co-operation of the Singapore government's Urban Redevelopment Authority for the land necessary to build the requisite number of carpark lots.

The OCBC Centre (Private) Limited, a wholly owned subsidiary responsible for the project, was formed and spearheaded by Goh Sin Tub, Assistant General Manager of OCBC, who headed the Control Committee of architects and consultants.

With the land parcels assembled, and the project managers appointed, Pei began work in earnest, using a local Singapore architectural firm, BEP Akitek, and the structural engineers Ove Arup & Partners, to execute his ideas. The China Building was demolished in 1971, and the bank set up temporary quarters in Upper Pickering Street.

The new building would forever change Singapore's skyline. At 650 feet, it was then the tallest building in Southeast Asia. The commanding OCBC Centre was to be one of superlatives. It boasted the largest banking hall in Southeast Asia, made of polished stainless steel, forty-feet tall and spanning almost 140 feet by 100 feet, without pillars. In order to create an area with no visual obstacles, Pei designed two fifty-two-storey towers, which formed the support for the banking hall. The hall's antique gold carpet was an enormous single piece — 4,000 square feet in size, the largest ever woven in Singapore. The carpet was brought to the building on a gigantic ten-wheel lorry and required thirty struggling workers to unroll it.

The new OCBC building was the first computerised banking facility in the region, housing an advanced foreign exchange, interbank local money exchange and Asian Currency Unit marketing office, all in one dealing room. Security, a bank's true currency, was exemplified by the vaults' doors, which could withstand water, fire, blow torches, or explosives. Another record for the region were the rows and rows of stainless steel safe deposit boxes — 10,000 in all — housed protectively beneath the magnificent four-storey banking hall, in a fireproof, watertight environment.

To efficiently serve the million square feet of space, the Otis Elevator Company was awarded the largest lift-installation contract for any single building in Southeast Asia, with a total of twenty-nine lifts, some of which could reach speeds of 1,200 feet per minute. On the roof, a helicopter pad was available in case of emergency.

The office tower gave the impression of imposing physical strength without coarseness. The solid concrete buttresses were separated on each facing side by three banks of windows containing more than 100,000 square feet of glass. Each glass section was thirteen stories high and was cantilevered out eighteen feet to convey a feeling of lightness.

The exterior of the building was clad in elegant Sardinian granite. At least, some of it was. When Pei offered samples of the potential exterior stonework, TCT had a choice between two kinds of granite, one cheaper and less durable, but superficially seemingly identical to the more expensive one. Pei preferred the Sardinian rock. TCT asked that both samples be placed side by side in the lunchroom and asked his employees to tell the difference. When they couldn't, TCT suggested that Pei use the more costly stone for the first fifty feet, then switch to the more economical stone for the remaining height, where it would not be subjected to close public scrutiny. The substitute stone saved the bank $10 million.

With his extensive experience in construction for Eastern Realty, Tan Chin Tuan became directly involved in almost every detail of the new building. He even personally chose the tenants. Demonstrating his finely honed common sense, he specifically excluded restaurants, stockbrokers and auctioneers, who would crowd the elevators with large numbers of casual visitors. Embassies were also discouraged, due to the potential risk of political demonstrations and international terrorism.

However, those accepted as tenants were well looked after. On the 33rd floor, there were special facilities known as the Executives' Club, containing exclusive dining rooms and executive lounges for the use of the member tenants. The 19th floor contained four small conference rooms and an ultra-modern conference facility, which could seat 200.

The top floors were reserved for the OCBC chairman, top management, advisers and VIPs. In addition, the 49th floor incorporated several boardrooms, including the principal boardroom, which contained a giant table with a map of Singapore in its centre.

The building was designed to accommodate 5,000 people. Several of the new tenants were OCBC-linked companies such as Great Eastern Life, SIMBL and SINGMAS. Other companies, whose chairmen were TCT's long-time associates and companies owned by OCBC's board members, such as Lee Rubber Co, asked to move in. Professional firms, consultants, petroleum and shipping corporations, insurance companies and twenty-five international banks took up tenancy at Singapore's most prestigious new address.

Construction of the substation commenced in 1971, preparing the way for the superstructure, which began in June 1973. The actual building was erected in remarkably short order — thirty-nine months. TCT organised the purchase of two cranes, so that work on the two cores could be continuous, twenty-four hours a day. During the height of the project, more than a thousand people worked on the office towers.

Initially, I.M. Pei had recommended a Japanese artist to produce a sculpture for the OCBC Square in front of OCBC Centre South. But as he was unavailable, the legendary English sculptor Henry Moore was contracted instead. Moore's superb (and initially controversial) Reclining Lady continues to grace the front entrance to this day.

The $100 million OCBC Centre was completed in September 1976. The official opening on October 1 was a day to remember. The celebrations began with a luncheon for 300 foreign guests and bankers at the Shangri-La Hotel. At 5 P.M., more than 3,000 guests gathered below the colourful flags and festive bunting adorning the glittering banking hall.

The distinguished guests were a who's who of the business community and government. They included the minister for national development Lim Kim San; Tun Tan Siew Sin (former Malaysian minister of finance) and his wife Toh Puan Tan Siew Sin; Tan Sri Nik Kamil (former deputy speaker of the Malaysian Parliament, Menteri Besar, [Chief Minister] of Kelantan, Malaysia's Permanent Representative to the United Nations and chairman of Rothmans (Malaysia)); Lord Armstrong of Sanderstead (former head of the United Kingdom's Home Civil Service); Sir John Prideaux (chairman of National Westminster Bank); as well as scores of chairmen, presidents and chief executives of local and international banks. One very proud guest was the building's architect, I. M. Pei. Thirty Singapore Girl Pipers and thirty-five Chin Woo lion dancers welcomed the guests, with a red carpet leading to a reception line headed by Tan Chin Tuan.

Two very special invited guests, dear to the chairman's heart, spoke at the inauguration, one in English, the other in Chinese. Dr Chang Kia Ngau, the doyen of Chinese bankers, and the Right Honourable Malcolm MacDonald (the former U.K. commissioner-general for Southeast Asia) addressed the assembly.

Dr Chang spoke of his forty-four-year friendship with the OCBC and his admiration for its chairman. In a message published in all Singapore newspapers, he paid tribute to Tan Chin Tuan:

> "...whose vision, dedication and integrity have been the driving forces behind the success of OCBC. I believe this magnificent building is a fitting monument to his leadership."

Malcolm MacDonald, in his speech to the assembled guests, likened the new OCBC Centre to the Parthenon in Athens. It was, as MacDonald explained, a fitting comparison. Both ancient Athens and modern Singapore were industrious, creative and influential city-states. And just as the Parthenon was one of the greatest examples of classical architecture, he declared the OCBC Centre one of the most handsome examples of modern architecture to be seen anywhere in the world.

MacDonald gently chided the chairman for omitting to mention a vital contributor to the project and proceeded to rectify the situation:

> "When the OCBC first came into being, during the worldwide economic depression in 1932, a young man named Tan Chin Tuan was appointed its secretary and assistant manager. Throughout the succeeding 44 years, he has played a brilliant part in guiding and leading the OCBC to its present position in the banking world.

> "He is indeed the principal architect and builder of the banking colossus which now inhabits this tower. Incidentally, the building's 52 storeys help to celebrate the 52 years through which he has actually been associated with Oversea-Chinese Banking... I do not need to tell this audience about the high importance which the OCBC has attained both inside and outside Singapore. I will only say that the Corporation has made a huge contribution to transforming Singapore from the economically dependent little colony that it was less than 20 years ago into the prosperously independent, internationally influential nation that it is today."

TCT's speech at the inauguration admitted that "since 1969, the OCBC Centre has been a magnificent obsession — not just an ordinary building project, but an all absorbing and demanding way of life for those of us involved with it".

Tan Chin Tuan is a master of understatement. As the man who had joined the Chinese Commercial Bank in the same location in 1925, built the China Building on the same site in 1932 and then oversaw its demolition to make way for the imposing structure being celebrated, he declared, "We are delighted to be back in our birthplace, somewhat enlarged over the last six decades."

Gracious and generous, his speech praised the government, the consultants, the contractors and the thousands of labourers responsible for the building. TCT then paid tribute to its architect. "My ambition has been to help build a strong and progressive financial institution worthy of the confidence of its constituents and capable of fully serving the big and small of these regions. Mr I.M. Pei of New York has successfully translated into concrete reality our corporate aims and image of lasting strength, continuous growth and uprightness in his conceptual design of OCBC's headquarters."

The chairman concluded with an announcement reflecting the benevolence his leadership inspired. He introduced the OCBC Centre Scholarships tenable at six regional colleges and universities, "to upgrade the skills and capabilities of the next generation and to commemorate this milestone in our onward march".

At the invitation of the chairman, the guests then took the elevators to the 50th floor, where they viewed the panorama below. Not only was there the magnificent spectacle of the developing city of 2.2 million below, but the elevation also gave a glimpse of Singapore's two neighbours, Malaysia and Indonesia.

At sundown, there were audible gasps from the assembly, as the lights from all fifty-two stories were illuminated. The building suddenly became a great gleaming beacon in the darkening sky. The Straits Times declared the new OCBC Centre could be seen "as far away as Indonesia".

Tan Chin Tuan quietly slipped away, to review the twinkling landscape below and privately savour how much had been accomplished in six short years. The OCBC Centre was not only the bank's sophisticated and dynamic new home, but also the lustrous symbol of its enduring faith in Singapore's future. The imposing building was the physical manifestation of the bank's legendary motto — standing tall and powerful against the horizon — as solid as a rock.

Retirement, Honours and Accolades

OCBC Centre, the concrete monument to the growth and success of OCBC, now dominated the skyline of Singapore. The bank had become a diversified world-class institution, offering a profusion of modern services. Its carefully honed management structure allowed for smooth and deliberate transitions within the organisation, with senior executives personally chosen and groomed by the chairman. Tan Chin Tuan was scrupulously preparing for his retirement.

But first, another golden anniversary had to be celebrated. The bank, founded so many decades before in a time of adversity, had reached its 50th year of operation in October 1982.

The Oversea-Chinese Banking Corporation had been established in 1932 with a capital of $10 million. Initially intended as a small organisation catering to the financial needs of local Chinese merchants, it had matured into an international banking power with forty-five branches throughout the world and a substantial portfolio of prominent and successful investments. OCBC was ranked among the top 500 banks in the world and its level of liquidity was the envy of the industry. By 1982, under Tan Chin Tuan's leadership, its capital had grown to $412 million and a decade later would soar to $716 million.

Between 1945, when TCT was appointed managing director, and

197

his retirement in 1983, shareholders funds had increased by more than $1 billion. A graph of OCBC's stunning profits showed a strong line rising steadily, from $3.09 million in 1946, to $117.79 million in 1983. Total assets had increased correspondingly to more than $10 billion. Shareholders were elated by the consistent dividends, which were usually in double digits and never less than 5 per cent annually in the entire post-war period. That still acceptable 5 per cent occurred during the difficult first years of post-war reconstruction.

OCBC enjoyed the respect of the public, the worldwide banking industry and the international financial press. *Asian Finance* hailed what it called OCBC's "solid pride of prudent banking". *Euromoney* noted that even during the high-rolling 1980s, a prudent OCBC enjoyed a profitability unmatched by other more adventurous institutions. Lim Mah Hui, a Professor at Temple University stated: "The name and influence of OCBC in Malaysia's and Singapore's economies is synonymous with that of the house of Morgan or Rockefeller in the United States."

The *Asian Wall Street Journal* described OCBC as a "Chinese bank that supports the little guy through thick and thin", inspiring "tremendous loyalty by depositors and clients". The lifeblood of any financial institution, the average depositor and investor, certainly appreciated OCBC's "solid as a rock" stability. Throughout a half century of depression, war, anti-colonial unrest, turbulent politics and the uncertainties of independence, the bank had protected the ordinary man, safeguarding his savings and increasing his investments. It was, as Tan Chin Tuan once called it, a sacred trust and a duty not to be taken lightly.

As part of the bank's 50th anniversary celebrations, a reception was held for the fifty longest-serving employees. Speaking on behalf of the board of directors, Lee Seng Wee singled out TCT's accomplishments:

> "Chairman Tan Sri Tan has not only helped to make history for the bank, he has also created history for himself.

198

"Firstly, he holds the distinction of having served the longest period in the bank. He therefore heads the group of the 'Gallant 50'. Secondly, he is presently the only link between one of the predecessor banks, the Chinese Commercial Bank, which he joined on 1st March 1925, and OCBC. Thirdly, he has been the youngest managing director of the Bank, having been appointed joint-managing director with the late Mr Tan Ean Kiam in February 1942, just before the fall of Singapore.

"Fourthly, he is so far the only serving officer in the bank to have risen from the ranks to hold the highest position in the bank as Chairman. Fifthly, under his Chairmanship and leadership, the bank has seen such tremendous progress to become one of the largest and strongest banks in this region. Sixthly, he was the only member of the bank to be appointed deputy president of the Singapore Legislative Council in 1951, the highest post that any local person could aspire to at the time.

"Lastly, and certainly not least, in terms of loyalty and dedication and devotion to the bank, I can say that there cannot be anyone who can excel him. Chairman Tan Sri Tan has certainly created a record, which will never be surpassed. We trust that he will always be blessed with good health so that he can lead the Bank for a long time to come."

But despite his entreaties to stay, Lee Seng Wee knew that Tan Chin Tuan was carefully preparing for retirement. At the anniversary celebration, TCT credited "the staunch support of shareholders, customers and associates; the dedication of management and staff; and a happy and harmonious board have all contributed to making the OCBC what it is today". However, all of those in attendance were acutely aware that the bank's extraordinary success was due to the guiding hand of one of Asia's outstanding business leaders. Now, with the bank as steadfast as the rock of Gibraltar and having passed half a century of prosperity, everything was scrupulously in place to allow that great man to step down.

On September 30, 1983, at eight o'clock in the evening, Tan Chin Tuan's banking career officially came to a close. On that historic night, he was escorted into the Shangri-La Hotel to be greeted by more than a thousand guests and bank employees, most of OCBC's Singapore staff and a twenty-nine-person choir all enthusiastically singing *For He's a Jolly Good Fellow*.

In recognition of his historic, lengthy and successful stewardship of the bank, the OCBC board of directors presented Tan Chin Tuan with a twenty-two-carat solid gold medallion, 4.5 inches in diameter. Weighing 1,000 grams, it bore on one side, the profile of the OCBC Centre, and on the other, the eponymous Chinese junk and the words "To commemorate 59 years of dedicated service".

The incoming chairman, Yong Pung How, put the occasion into perspective:

"For more than half a century now, OCBC has played a prominent part in the local banking scene. And for as long as anyone of us can remember, Tan Sri Tan has been not just the managing director or the chairman of OCBC, he has been OCBC."

Lee Seng Wee spoke on behalf of the board of directors:

"We are gathered here tonight to honour the man who is our last link with the beginnings of our bank, who through most of this period has guided its destiny, repairing the ravages of the Second World War, dealing with the political changes that followed as two nations moved towards independence, building up our bank from its minor, colonial status into the sturdy and powerful institution known and respected world-wide.

"This is the great achievement of Tan Sri Tan Chin Tuan. A few simple figures will show the magnitude of this achievement. In 1945, when he was made sole managing director, the shareholders funds of OCBC stood at less than $15 million. In 1966, when he assumed the chairmanship, they had risen to $70 million. Today, they are in excess of $1.1 billion. But more important is that such rapid growth was achieved while maintaining full security for the bank and its depositors, so that the OCBC is in as good a position as any bank in the world to weather the storms that may loom ahead in these uncertain times. The best measure of the high esteem and confidence that the investing public has in the OCBC and its chairman is our market capitalisation, which now stands at an astonishing $5.3 billion, more than that of the Midland and Westpac banks put together!

"Later on, you will hear many testimonials to all the sterling virtues that have enabled Tan Sri Tan to accomplish so much. I shall content myself with mentioning some of his more unusual qualities — unusual in the context of the local business environment. As we all know, he has always maintained the highest standards of personal integrity, foregoing numerous opportunities for personal profit. His scrupulous adherence to principle is proverbial, often courting unpopularity when he had to turn down requests for favours from friends. His total and selfless devotion to OCBC meant that he always put the interests of the bank above his own."

In a long and moving speech on behalf of the staff, Mr Teo Cheng Guan described Tan Chin Tuan:

"His brilliant mind appears to work best under pressure. He thrives on challenges. Cool, calm and unfluttered, he has always come up with a right solution. The success of the bank has been due in no small measure to his uncanny foresight and intuition... If I may borrow the words of Winston Churchill, seldom has so much been owed by so many to a single person... You will always be remembered for your dynamic leadership; for your fair-mindedness, patience, understanding and forebearance; for your very high standards of integrity, dedication, honour and loyalty. Above all, we shall always remember you as a true and genuine friend and an excellent mentor. We shall always cherish our long and happy association with you."

Confirming the affection that was felt for the chairman, the choir sang *May the Good Lord Bless and Keep You*. Now it was time for Tan Chin Tuan to address the gathering. Approaching the podium with a composure that camouflaged his true feelings, he shared his private thoughts with the assembled guests and friends:

"If a banker is supposed to have no emotions, I must confess that tonight I am no banker at all. What has been said is sufficient to rock even a rock."

In a speech filled with warmth, humour, modesty and gratitude, TCT generously remembered and acknowledged his mentors, predecessors, colleagues and staff. The celebration ended with the choir's emotional rendering of *Auld Lang Syne*.

Although his official career ended that evening, an appreciative board of directors conferred on TCT the lifetime title of honorary president. The board had attempted to offer TCT compensation to cover the early years after the war when he was paid a pittance, but TCT declined, fearing the gesture would set a burdensome precedent for the bank.

He did, however, accept the bank's offer of the continued exclusive use of the offices he had called home for nine years — the 49th floor of the OCBC Centre.

By remaining in his OCBC offices, TCT would continue to be available to staff, managers and directors to provide advice concerning policy or management matters. Bank director Lee Seng Wee assured them, "Though formally retired, he will continue to serve our bank in a different but still very useful capacity, hopefully for many more years than the 59 recorded so far."

In addition to the deserved accolades for his many accomplishments, the celebration provided an opportunity to look back on a momentous career and an equally remarkable life. Tan Sri Tan Chin Tuan had lived, and continues to live, a full life; indeed, he has actually managed three successful careers — as a pioneering legislator, as an important banker and as a leader of a highly successful business conglomerate.

TCT had tried to retire over the years. But his intentions were often thwarted. The talented men he had carefully nurtured as potential successors ended up being recruited into public service by the Singapore Government. His message to shareholders in the 1982 OCBC annual report, his last as chairman, referred to this fact:

> "I have sought and planned over the last 15 years or so to shed my onerous burden of responsibilities, but carefully laid plans were frustrated time and again by the loss of senior personnel who had been groomed for future leadership of the bank."

One of these key men was Mr Yong Pung How, a Cambridge University-educated lawyer from Malaysia. Experienced and highly regarded in industry and banking, he moved down from Kuala Lumpur in 1971 to be chairman and managing director of the newly created Singapore

International Merchant Bankers Ltd in which OCBC held a majority stake.

A year later, he was appointed to the boards of OCBC and Straits Trading Company. In 1973, he became a director of Wearne Brothers as well. In 1977, he was appointed vice-chairman of OCBC.

In 1981, the Monetary Authority of Singapore was revamping its investment portfolio. It asked Mr Yong to head its newly formed Government of Singapore Investment Corporation, and the following year, he became managing director of MAS.

It was only in 1983 that he was available to relieve Tan Chin Tuan as OCBC chairman. Mr Yong remained chairman till 1989, when he was appointed a judge in the Supreme Court and became Chief Justice a year later on Chief Justice Wee Chong Jin's retirement.

Another of the high-calibre men whom Tan Chin Tuan was nurturing to succeed him was his nephew, Dr Tony Tan Keng Yam. Highly educated, with three degrees, Dr Tan had a successful career in academia as a senior lecturer at the local university. But in 1969, he decided to join the bank.

Dr Tan quickly made his mark in the bank, in particular his effective handling of the computerisation of OCBC's banking processes, and so was promoted to the post of general manager.

However, like Mr Yong, Dr Tan too was required to do "national" service for a rapidly growing nation. Lee Kuan Yew, the then prime minister, requested that Dr Tan be seconded to help reorganise Singapore's public transportation system.

After that assignment, he returned to OCBC. But after having worked with PM Lee, he was urged to go into politics. He consulted TCT, and in February 1979, he was elected to Parliament as the Member for Sembawang constituency and was appointed Senior Minister of State (Education).

In June 1980, he was appointed Minister for Education and, concurrently, the Vice-Chancellor of the National University of Singapore. From 1981 to 1991, he held various portfolios, including Education, Trade and Industry, Finance and Health.

In December 1991, Dr Tan stepped down from the Cabinet to return to the private sector as OCBC's chairman and chief executive officer. He, however, remained a Member of Parliament. In 1995, he rejoined the Government as Deputy Prime Minister and Minister for Defence.

Although TCT realised that he should make generous sacrifices for the greater benefit of the nation, these departures meant he had to continue deferring his retirement even as he sought repeatedly to retire.

Just as he prepared competent men to succeed him at the bank, TCT also nurtured talent in the other key companies within the OCBC group, likening his development of skilful individuals to his hobby of growing orchids. "When I grow a perfect bloom, I feel happy," he declared.

TCT's successor at Fraser and Neave was Michael Fam, whose career was varied and successful. Fam had studied engineering in Australia and later became a prominent executive. In addition to his appointment as executive chairman of F&N, Fam assumed the chairmanships of Asia Pacific Breweries, Centrepoint Properties and Carnaud Metalbox Asia. He also serves as director of Oversea-Chinese Banking Corporation Limited and Singapore Press Holdings Limited. His career in public service is equally distinguished: he chaired the Housing and Development Board, Public Transport Council, Public Sector Divestment Committee and Nanyang Technological University Council. One of Fam's outstanding accomplishments was overseeing the construction of Singapore's Mass Rapid Transit system in the early 1980s. TCT said of Mr Fam: "It makes me very happy to have collaborated with a man of his calibre."

Tan Chin Tuan also retired as chairman of Wearne Brothers and Malayan Breweries, secure in the knowledge that the men he had put in place would continue to nurture the businesses as carefully as he had. However, at Straits Trading Company and Great Eastern Life, he remained chairman until 1992. Although he offered to step down at the shareholders' meeting each year, the boards passed unanimous resolutions requesting that TCT stay on.

At Great Eastern Life, the board minutes recorded Lee Seng Wee's remarks, "that the Company has enlarged to be the biggest life insurance company in the region, not only in terms of size but also in reputation, financial strength and in almost every way — owed in no small measure to our Chairman". Great Eastern Life's directors gratefully appointed TCT honorary life president.

Straits Trading Company also registered similar displays of regret at TCT's departure and similarly conferred on him the designation of honorary life president, as did every one of the other corporations he formerly chaired.

Tan Chin Tuan created significant wealth for his companies and its shareholders. The statistics illustrate a considerable increase in the value of shareholders' funds from the date of his initial appointment as director to his retirement as chairman. Malayan Breweries (now Asia Pacific Breweries) increased 1,633 per cent ($194,000,000); Fraser and Neave expanded by 2,632 per cent ($289,600,000); Overseas Assurance's values were raised by 2,703 per cent ($38,770,000); Robinson and Co. grew from $4,000,000 to $56,000,000; and Wearne Brothers increased 403 per cent ($251,000,000). During TCT's tenure as chairman, Great Eastern Life increased 1,233 per cent ($225,600,000); and Straits Trading Company grew by 1,502 per cent ($691,962,000).

This extraordinary growth was achieved by a man who had been so scrupulously honest in his business dealings that there was not one breath of scandal, or suggestion of misdoing throughout his entire career. A man whose very name was synonymous with honour and integrity.

Now that the corporations he nurtured had passed into reliable hands, TCT could devote more of his attention to activities that mean a lot to him. He had no qualms about the future. "I am looking ahead. When people retire, they sometimes worry they won't have something to do. For me, retirement is just shedding some of the load off my right shoulder. My left shoulder still has quite a burden."

He now had the time for personal business ventures, hobbies and pastimes, charity work and thoughtful reflection. He could enjoy many of his life's pleasures — exquisite cuisine, growing orchids, his birds and his horses. A keen racing enthusiast, TCT was elected chairman of the Singapore Turf Club in 1983. At the time, one newspaper noted: "Mr Tan belongs to a fast-vanishing breed of racehorse owners who genuinely loves horses, win or lose, and race for the fun of it."

He had first shown an interest in horses in the late 1950s, sharing this hobby with his wife, Helene. Their first champion was Happy Melody, a fast Irish gelding that won the King's Gold Cup in 1959, and the Summer Cup and Stewards Cup in 1960. Some of his favourite winning horses included Automation, which swept the Singapore Cup and the Penang Gold Cup in 1960; Towkay, victor of the Queen Elizabeth II Cup in 1981; and Tuneful Melody, which won the first Raffles Cup in 1991.

TCT shared his passion for horses with his wide circle of friends, including many of the region's most prominent citizens. One was Malaysia's first prime minister, Tunku Abdul Rahman. Often, when TCT was in Kuala Lumpur on business, he and the Tunku would get together to break bread and exchange ideas. When Tan Chin Tuan became interested in horse racing, the friends decided to co-invest in a thoroughbred. Tan Chin Tuan asked the Tunku to choose a name for their first horse, which he did in honour of their relationship — True Friendship. Later, TCT shared two other horses, Setia Kawan and Setia Kawan II, with the Tunku. This time he chose their names. In Malay, *Setia Kawan* also means "true friendship".

Another of TCT's pleasurable and enduring hobbies is his interest in birds. Despite the deterioration in his hearing, he could discern and enjoy their tuneful singing. One of his favourites, a grey parrot, perks up immediately when it hears his voice. Bending its head, wishing to be stroked, it responds to his voice with an inquisitive "How are you?" TCT also keeps melodious Sharma birds and has won best-of-show with them in competitions. To encourage them to sing, he plays tape recordings of other sharmas, filling the room with the joyous merging of electronic and live bird song.

A patron of the Society for the Prevention of Cruelty to Animals, TCT is fond of all animals, and his home is filled with dogs of varying sizes, shapes and ages. However, a special place in his heart is reserved for Alsatians (also known as German Shepherd Dogs), a breed known for their devotion and vigilance.

Orchids are another of TCT's passions and The Orchid Society of South East Asia has enjoyed his patronage. His interest in orchids germinated from an act of kindness many years previously. Shortly after the war, a merchant named Tan Siew Kwa requested a loan to import musical instruments. TCT agreed and the man prospered. A decade later, in gratitude for helping him start his business, Tan Siew Kwa asked TCT's permission to name a new orchid after him, resulting in the elegant Vanda Tan Chin Tuan. Thereafter, TCT developed an interest in growing orchids and filled his gardens with these magnificent flowers.

Still, TCT's passion burns brightest when it comes to helping others, such as being Patron of YMCA (Singapore). However, his generosity to individuals and associations has been mostly unheralded, because he prefers the most dignified and meaningful form of charity — that of giving anonymously. He established the Tan Foundation to distribute funds to a wide variety of organisations. The beneficiaries include dozens of children's charities, educational institutions, hospitals, and other altruistic and humanitarian associations.

Like his father and Tan Kah Kee before him, TCT has been a great benefactor to all levels of Singaporean education. Commemorating the teachers and principals who made such a difference to his young life, he provided scholarships to the Anglo-Chinese School in their names, to assist successive generations. The school has also benefited from a variety of sports facilities, auditoriums and indeed, entire buildings, all donated by its most prominent alumnus, Tan Chin Tuan.

Celebrating the golden jubilee of the Anglo-Chinese School, Reverend P.L. Peach recalled the incident when he had to intervene and choose whether or not to allow TCT to retake the Junior Cambridge examination. "Chin Tuan had a hard decision to make in 1922, and so did I," he remembered. "What impresses me now is that the perseverance and ambition of this young man, coupled with a right decision of a Principal, have both ended in a life of great service to his people and the business world."

Tan Chin Tuan champions higher education not only in Singapore but also abroad. In 1984, he donated $1 million to the Needham Research Institute, one of the world's top three centres for Chinese science and technology. The funds were used for the construction and equipping of the East Asian History of Science Library in Cambridge, England. In a letter to the project's director, Cambridge professor Dr Joseph Needham, TCT wrote, "I am very happy to be able to contribute towards the perpetuation of the study of Chinese culture, on which you have devoted so much of your life's efforts." A plaque in the library building commemorates TCT's generous contribution, pivotal to the project's completion.

In his letter of appreciation to Tan Chin Tuan, Dr Needham replied, "It is particularly auspicious that Singaporean Chinese culture should be thus associated. China has been profoundly misjudged by the Western world in the past, but this will no longer be the case in time to come."

TCT also supported worthy institutions such as the Salk Institute for Biological Studies of La Jolla, California. The research institute is one of the world's most important academic organisations in the field of biological sciences. Elected to the institute's International Council in 1981, TCT was given the responsibility to act as a regional ambassador for the Salk Institute, to stay informed on current research topics and to attend seminars on those subjects.

Over the years, TCT made generous donations to the Salk Institute and, working with the Singapore Turf Club, helped Singapore scientists with funding for training at the institute.

The fact that he didn't have the opportunity for higher education never rankled TCT, who liked to joke that he had "no alphabets after my name", referring to the initials found after the names of university graduates. But while he may not have had the extended tertiary education that others enjoyed (he always humbly claimed that he advanced as far as he did thanks to good luck), his lifetime of achievement resulted in many honorary titles and degrees.

In recognition of his contribution to the National University of Singapore, to public service and to banking, Singapore's President and University Chancellor Wee Kim Wee awarded TCT with an honorary degree of Doctor of Laws in 1991.

Another honour bestowed on Tan Chin Tuan reverberated with the gratifying echoes of the past. In June 1992, to commemorate his distinguished leadership in international banking and business, Curtin University of Australia conferred on TCT the honorary degree of Doctor of Letters. The university was named for the Right Honourable John Curtin, the prime minister who had guided Australia through World War II, and the man who had shown TCT such kindness and consideration during his initial visit to Canberra in 1941.

In his acceptance speech, TCT commended the wartime generosity of that country's prime minister and the officials of the Bank of New South Wales (now Westpac), who personified the values he most cherished. "This and other kindnesses... revealed to me the true Australian character — a generous nature and remarkable sense of fair play."

In a citation given at the ceremony, the Honourable Ian Taylor, Vice-Premier of Western Australia declared:

"You are, Sir, a living legend, epitomising the astonishing and remarkable development of Singapore, not only as a regional banking centre, but as a leading banking, financial, business and communications city of the world... I make special mention of this, Sir, because we recognise you as a practical, as well as a very friendly link between our countries and economies."

Professor John Maloney, Vice-Chancellor of Curtin University, also observed:

"Tan Sri's commitment, abilities, personal and professional integrity, symbolise not only the qualities of an enormously successful city state and people, but they cross all borders and foster levels of confidence and trust which are assured of being in ever increasing demand... The achievement of leaders such as Tan Sri Tan in what they have created in their profession and country, in what they have done for international banking and business or their professions, is a matter in which all of us can take pride and for which all of us can be grateful."

Now honoured by Singapore, Malaysia, Australia and Great Britain, and adding these doctorates to his CBE and Panglima Setia Mahkota, Tan Sri Dr Tan Chin Tuan experienced tangible proof of the international esteem in which he was held.

Today, TCT maintains an active daily schedule. He continues to follow the OCBC group's activities with interest, offering advice when asked, providing direction where needed. A lifelong gourmet, he hosts delicious luncheons daily, carefully planning every detail of the menu for his favoured guests. He carefully keeps abreast of national and international news events, and the state of financial markets worldwide. And he devotes time each day to his charities, initiating kind and thoughtful deeds.

Caring for the elderly remains one particular area of compassion. The Tan Foundation gives generously to many homes for the aged, including the Little Sisters of the Poor, to provide Christmas dinners and other benefits. Tan Chin Tuan himself has privately visited many residences for the elderly, quietly distributing red packets to the residents.

Although his donations are usually anonymous, on the occasion of his 91st birthday, which coincided with Senior Citizen's Week, he made a rare conspicuous public gift. To celebrate his own nine decades of vitality and to reward "active ageing", Tan Chin Tuan promised a generous offer of $1,000 to every vigorous, still active Singaporean citizen over the age of ninety. He placed no cap or restrictions on the number of people who could receive the endowment, which was given simply because he felt lucky and blessed, and wished to share his good fortune with others over the age of ninety.

TCT believes people exist to mutually benefit one another. With an irrefutable reputation for benevolence, he has time and again seen good deeds that he initiated, flow back and forth, like the tides that wash over Singapore's coastal shores, enriching everyone in the process.

The extraordinary life of Tan Sri Dr Tan Chin Tuan is a metaphor for the nation he helped to build. From humble beginnings, Singapore has matured into a country of international significance. Tan Chin Tuan's contributions to his country as a banker, a businessman, a legislator and a public benefactor, may never be fully appreciated. His life and work serve as an example of diligence, dedication and generosity. What cannot be refuted is that, in the end, he made the world a better place.

Index